Oral Language and Early Literacy in Preschool

Talking, Reading, and Writing

2ND EDITION

KATHLEEN A. ROSKOS
PATTON O. TABORS
LISA A. LENHART

Part of the Preschool Literacy Collection edited by
Lesley Mandel Morrow

INTERNATIONAL Reading Association

800 BARKSDALE ROAD, PO BOX 8139
NEWARK, DE 19714-8139, USA
www.reading.org

Executive Editor, Books   Corinne M. Mooney
Developmental Editor   Charlene M. Nichols
Developmental Editor   Tori Mello Bachman
Developmental Editor   Stacey L. Reid
Editorial Production Manager   Shannon T. Fortner
Design and Composition Manager   Anette Schuetz
Project Editor   Stacey L. Reid

Cover   Design, Monotype; Photograph, ©2009 Jupiterimages Corporation

Library of Congress Cataloging-in-Publication Data
Roskos, Kathy.
   Oral language and early literacy in preschool : talking, reading, and writing / Kathleen A. Roskos, Patton O. Tabors, and Lisa A. Lenhart. — 2nd ed.
       p. cm. — (Preschool literacy collection)
   Includes bibliographical references and index.
   ISBN 978-0-87207-693-8
1. Children—Language.   2. Oral communication.   3. Reading (Early childhood)   4. Language arts (Early childhood)   I. Tabors, Patton O. II. Lenhart, Lisa A.   III. Title.
   LB1139.L3R675 2008
   372.62'2--dc22   2008046564

CONTENTS

 Kathleen Roskos, PhD, teaches courses in pre-K–12 reading education at John Carroll University in University Heights, Ohio, USA. Formerly an elementary classroom teacher, Roskos has served in a variety of administrative roles, including director of federal programs in the public schools, department chair in higher education, and director of the Ohio Literacy Initiative at the Ohio Department of Education from 2000 to 2002. She has developed and coordinated numerous educational grants that provide services to classroom teachers and children. She designed and coordinated one of the first public preschools in Ohio (Bridges and Links). She has been instrumental in the design and development of more than a dozen online professional development learning modules in literacy for pre-K–12 teachers.

Roskos studies early literacy development, teacher cognition, and the design of professional education for teachers. She has published several books, book chapters, and research articles on these topics. Her most recent books include *Nurturing Knowledge: Building a Foundation for School Success by Linking Early Literacy to Math, Science, Art, and Social Studies*, coauthored with Susan B. Neuman (2007), *Designing Professional Development in Literacy: A Framework for Effective Instruction*, coauthored with Catherine A. Rosemary and Leslie K. Landreth (2007), and *Play and Literacy in Early Childhood: Research From Multiple Perspectives* (second edition), coedited with James F. Christie (2007). New book chapters focus on literacy environment design ("The Benefits of Going Green") and new technologies in early learning ("The eBook as a Learning Object in an Online World").

Roskos presents and consults extensively in schools on topics of literacy curriculum development, early reading assessment, and teacher professional development in reading. She currently serves on the International Reading Association Standards 2010 Committee as a lead writer. She also serves on the Literacy Coaching Clearinghouse Advisory Council.

Patton O. Tabors, EdD, retired in 2005 as principal research associate at the Harvard Graduate School of Education. Prior to beginning her doctoral studies at the Harvard Graduate School of Education in 1981, Tabors was an elementary school teacher and a childbirth educator. Her doctoral studies focused on first- and second-language acquisition in young children. Her dissertation research described the developmental pathways of a group of young children learning English as a second language, which she later wrote about in *One Child, Two Languages: A Guide for Early Childhood Educators of Children Learning English as a Second Language* (1997, 2008).

From 1987 until 2003, Tabors was the research coordinator of the Home–School Study of Language and Literacy Development in collaboration with Catherine E. Snow and David K. Dickinson. She and Dickinson coedited *Beginning Literacy With Language: Young Children Learning at Home and School* (2001), which was based on the study's findings about the relationship between early childhood interactions and kindergarten language and literacy skills. More recently, Tabors coauthored, with Catherine E. Snow, Michelle V. Porche, and Stephanie Ross Harris, *Is Literacy Enough? Pathways to Academic Success for Adolescents* (2007), which explains factors beyond K–3 literacy that influenced students' later school success in the Home–School Study of Language and Literacy Development.

In 2000, Tabors became the principal investigator of a longitudinal project, the Early Childhood Study of Language and Literacy Development of Spanish-Speaking Children, which followed a sample of more than 300 bilingual children from preschool to second grade. With her colleagues Mariela M. Páez and Lisa M. López, she has used the findings from this study to continue to inform the ongoing discussion about young children and second-language and literacy acquisition.

Lisa A. Lenhart is a professor of education at the University of Akron in Akron, Ohio, USA. She is currently codirector of the Reading First Ohio Center for Professional Development and Technical Assistance and is director of e-Read Ohio. For the past several years she has been engaged in creating online professional development for teachers. Prior to her work at the University of Akron, she taught in Ohio's schools for more than 10 years. She is a coauthor of *Reading and Learning to Read*, a popular textbook in the field.

PREFACE

Much of what we learn in our lifetimes is by way of speaking, listening, reading, and writing. These are the symbolic tools that make us human; they help us to tell our stories. For this fundamental reason, it is important for preschool teachers to learn all they can about language and literacy development in the early years. What these teachers know and do makes a difference in the quality of early learning, which can build the foundations for their students' language development for life.

This book examines oral language and its first links to reading and writing. Its purpose is to share what we know from research about the role of oral language in children's early literacy development. Children's speaking and listening skills lead the way for their reading and writing skills, and together these language skills are the primary tools of the mind for all future learning. Please note that we use the term *oral language* to refer to speaking and listening and the term *literacy* to refer to reading and writing.

We use the word *talk* to indicate the skills of both speaking and listening. We focus on children who are 3 and 4 years old and who spend time in child care, Head Start, and preschool settings. We know that all preschool educators want to ensure young children a strong start in school readiness, and our goal is to provide them with the knowledge they need to create high-quality language- and literacy-learning environments.

This book has six chapters. It is written primarily for preschool teachers who make everyday decisions about the following:

- What oral language skills children need to learn
- What kinds of language and literacy experiences to provide
- What to look for in programs and materials
- Whether children are making progress in their use of language

Others interested in the education and development of young children—education leaders, school administrators, and parents—may find specific chapters informative. For our preschool teachers and teacher assistants, though, we encourage reading the entire book to learn more about joining language and early literacy in the early childhood classroom.

Please note that while Shelley Adams (featured in Chapter 6) is a real teacher, and all quotes and classroom dialogue offered in Chapter 6 are taken directly from Shelley's classroom, all other names used in this book are pseudonyms. Descriptions of students and teachers are composite sketches that represent real classroom situations that we have encountered in our studies.

CHAPTER 1

Joining Oral Language and Early Literacy

Oral language is the foundation of learning to read and write. Speaking and listening skills learned in the preschool years are crucial to future reading and writing achievement and school success. Children who do not develop strong oral language skills during this time find it difficult to keep pace with their peers in later years. They start to fall behind even before they start school (Biemiller, 2006; Hart & Risley, 2003; Scarborough, 2001; Snow, Burns, & Griffin, 1998).

In the preschool years all children need to learn to use language a lot. They need to learn how to carry on a good conversation with adults and peers. From age 3 onward, they should build a vocabulary store of at least 2,500 words per year (Biemiller & Slonim, 2001). They should encounter and explore at least two to four new words each day. They need to learn how to attend and listen on purpose (Blair, 2002).

Overall, young children need to develop skills in the following five primary areas of oral language.

1. *Semantics*: Developing meanings for the words children hear and say in their conversations with others.

2. *Syntax* (also known as grammar): Learning the rules of how words are linked together.

3. *Morphology*: Figuring out how to manipulate the smallest units of meaning in the language called morphemes. The word *preschool*, for example, has two morphemes: *Pre* (meaning *before*) and *school*.

4. *Phonology*: Understanding the sound structure of language. From birth onward (or even before) children are learning all the sounds or phonemes of their language.

5. *Pragmatics*: Understanding the social uses of language and basic social rules like saying "hello" and "goodbye," saying "please" and "thank you," and taking turns in a conversation.

With adults' help, children rapidly develop their language skills across the preschool years, and together these skills form the oral language foundation for effective communication over a lifetime (see Figure 1).

It is through their everyday experiences that children gain the oral language skills they need to become strong readers and learners in the future. From their parents and other adults in their lives, as well as their peers, children learn words, which they then use to learn more words and to build concepts about words and the world. Lacking exposure to rich language experiences, children can rapidly lose ground in their word learning and the word gap between them and their peers can widen substantially by the age of 4 (Hart & Risley, 2003).

For children with too little exposure to and development of oral language, learning to read and write is very hard. It is essential, therefore, that in their early years all children are exposed to an abundance of language in their everyday lives. Still, it is not enough for children to learn language on their own. It is important that they are helped to learn language in structured activities, such as shared reading, word play, and dramatic play. Children need time, resources, and multisensory learning opportunities to develop the oral language skills they need for school.

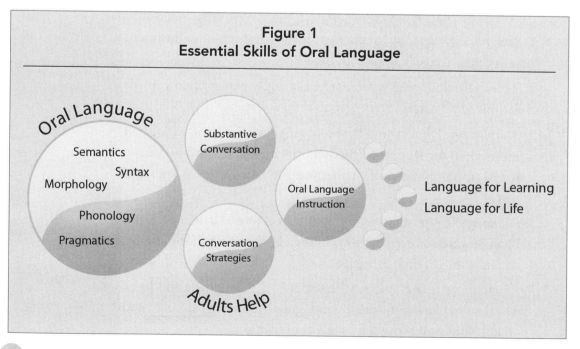

Figure 1
Essential Skills of Oral Language

A Framework for Joining Oral Language and Early Literacy

In achieving literacy, young children need writing to help them learn about reading, they need reading to help them learn about writing, and they need oral language to help them learn about both. Figure 2 presents a framework that shows how oral language and early literacy join to strengthen children's school readiness. Before they go to school, children need to develop oral language comprehension for listening and speaking, vocabulary for building background knowledge, phonological awareness and alphabet knowledge to attend to the structure and sounds of language, and print knowledge to develop concepts about books and printed words.

> In achieving literacy, young children need writing to help them learn about reading, they need reading to help them learn about writing, and they need oral language to help them learn about both.

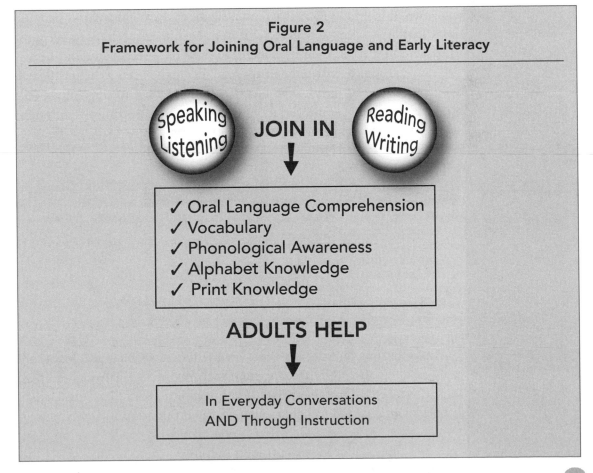

Figure 2
Framework for Joining Oral Language and Early Literacy

Speaking Listening   JOIN IN   Reading Writing

✓ Oral Language Comprehension
✓ Vocabulary
✓ Phonological Awareness
✓ Alphabet Knowledge
✓ Print Knowledge

ADULTS HELP

In Everyday Conversations
AND Through Instruction

Early childhood teachers need to intentionally plan language learning experiences that help children go beyond what they already know and can do.

Early childhood teachers need to intentionally plan language learning experiences that help children go beyond what they already know and can do. They need to develop children's oral language by creating conditions for them to learn through everyday conversations, and through instruction that includes guided participation, scaffolding, and practice opportunities to use language effectively. When teachers plan and deliberately create environments for language learning that are rich, appropriate, *and* enjoyable all children benefit.

For this to happen, early educators need to be planful, purposeful, and playful in their daily interaction with young children (Assel, Landry, Swank, & Gunnewig, 2007). In making plans for children's learning, educators need to consider what children already know and can do, and then take steps to further children's oral language comprehension. When purposeful, they set clear learning goals for children and deliberately engage them in activities that help them to explore language and develop the language skills they need. And when adults' language exchanges and interactions are playful, this appeals to children, encouraging them to use new words and to exercise their oral language skills in different situations.

Several sound instructional approaches can be used to help children explore, learn, and use oral language in the preschool years. These approaches can be used in a variety of early childhood settings—from prekindergartens to child-care centers to home-based care. Equally effective with whole and small groups of children as well as individual children, they include the following:

- Shared book reading
- Songs rhymes and word play
- Storytelling
- Circle time
- Dramatic play

Adaptations for young learners with special needs and talents can easily be integrated into these instructional approaches. Throughout this book, special attention will be paid to young children learning English as a second language. Given that language is the foundation for literacy, it is important to think how both first- and second-language development work for young children who come from homes where English is not the primary language.

Exploring the Framework

In the following chapters we help you explore this "joining" framework that connects oral language and early literacy in young children's preschool experiences. Building children's oral language foundation is at the core of a high-quality preschool literacy curriculum. Young children, especially those at risk, need supportive learning environments that nurture language and literacy. All children benefit from multisensory experiences that develop their expressive and receptive language skills so that they can share their ideas, tell their thoughts, listen, and ask questions for purposes of communication and understanding (New Standards Speaking and Listening Committee, 2001). Books, pencils, paper, and computers are literacy tools they can use to support and stimulate their language use in the pursuit of meaning. Together—that is, combined, conjoined, coincident—oral language and literacy help children grow and flourish in a changing world.

In our effort to clearly join language and literacy in the early years, the chapter that follows clarifies terminology and key concepts in the oral language learning domain. A shared vocabulary provides us with a common ground for talking about what we want to accomplish in developing children's oral language. It's important that we have an accurate description of what we mean by such terms as *phonological awareness*, *speech*, and *talk*. Terms such as these describe the connecting ideas that are essential for understanding oral language in the preschool curriculum and its role in early literacy.

In Chapter 3, planning—a key element in effective preschool instruction—is discussed. As stated earlier in this chapter, teachers need to be planful, and Chapter 3 demonstrates the importance of being intentional about the learning activities offered to children. The intentional teacher assesses to see where children are, using this information to plan and adjust instruction to meet children's needs. Planning helps teachers to make the best use of her resources, such as time, materials, and other adults who work closely with her in the classroom. It also helps teachers to stay on course toward meeting the oral language learning goals of the diverse children in the classroom. Well-drawn plans pave the way for lots of talk opportunities.

So what is needed for lots of talk opportunities? As Loris Malaguzzi, the famous founder of the program in Reggio Emilia, wrote, "To start with…there is the environment…a mechanism combining places, roles and functions… within a network of cooperation and interactions that produces for children a feeling of belonging in a world that is alive, welcoming and authentic" (Edwards, Gandini, & Forman, 1998, p. 64). In other words, a supportive learning environment creates the time and place for lots of talk.

Therefore, in Chapters 4 and 5, we discuss how teachers can achieve this setting. First, we discuss features that combine to produce a rich talk environment where language and early literacy are joined experiences. We describe several key concepts of oral language teaching in Chapter 4, including frameworks for conversation, conversation strategies, and oral language instructional activities. Then, in Chapter 5, we turn to best practices that ensure strong connections between oral language and early literacy. Best practices develop from research evidence, as well as professional wisdom distilled from teaching experience. How to routinely use best practices in oral language instruction goes to the heart of this book. Five instructional approaches are described in some detail regarding their rationale, protocols, procedures, and connections to standards frameworks. Real classroom examples are provided through the lens of an authentic lesson plan. Our goal in this chapter is to get at the details of adult–child interactions, which can make the difference between a satisfactory oral language experience and a spectacular one that is integrative, meaningful, and memorable for children.

Finally, Chapter 6 uses the example of Shelley Adams's preschool classroom as a way to demonstrate how the key components of integrating oral language and early literacy, as discussed in the preceding five chapters, all come together. We can observe—from the moment the children arrive to the time when they depart—how she provides appealing, sound, standards-based learning experiences that join children's oral language and early literacy skills. Shelley models the planful, purposeful, playful preschool teacher and early childhood educator who helps young children acquire and use language for learning.

In addition, we offer an Appendix that we call "My ABCs." This is a "one-stop shop" for quickly locating information about assessments (A), books (B), and curricular resources (C) that you can use to improve your language and literacy program. We are always on the lookout for high-quality resources that engage children in experiences where they can talk, read, and write a lot, and we want to pass our finds along to you.

FOR FURTHER EXPLORATION

Audiotape the language of two or three preschoolers engaged in a similar activity at the sand table, in dramatic play, or in project. Transcribe and analyze a portion of the language sample. Note the children's use of vocabulary, grammar, sentence complexity, and pragmatics. What conclusions can you draw about their language use?

CHAPTER 2

Understanding Terms and Fundamental Concepts

How children develop language is a topic of intense study. Over decades, much has been learned about this remarkable process, far more than we could ever discuss in one small book; however, familiarity with a few basic terms and fundamental concepts about language and early literacy will help you plan stimulating oral language experiences for children and communicate more clearly with fellow teachers and parents.

Nearly all the terms and concepts presented in this chapter are useful when thinking about any language system, not just English. Two exceptions apply: (1) Not all languages have a written form, and (2) some languages that are written do not use an alphabet or do not have an alphabet that is composed of 26 letters. All languages start with a group of sounds that must be learned and used by the infants in the families that speak that language. All languages have words that are made up of a variety of those sounds, and all conversation in all languages is made up of a group of words put together to express an idea. Communication in any language involves expressing and receiving ideas in a way that is understandable for all the people involved in the communication.

For young children who come from homes where English is not the primary language, all of these skills will have been developed in their home language. They will have learned the sounds of their language, the words of their language, and how to put words together to form ideas. So these young children will already know a great deal about how language works. They will bring those skills to the task of learning a new language; but it is important to remember that these children will need to start again with the sounds and the words of their new language, and with the rules about how conversation works in this language. This is a very big job for young children. See also *Preschool English Learners: Principles and Practices to Promote Language, Literacy, and Learning* (California Department of Education, 2007), a resource guide that helps teachers understand the preschool

English learner more fully. It offers principles and practices that promote language development, literacy, and learning among preschool English learners.

Key Terms

The following definitions are a useful introduction to several foundational concepts about language and early literacy that will be discussed later in the book. Our brief review of key terminology and concepts about language and literacy describes the important relationships between them. Defining key terms and explaining key concepts shows how oral language and preschool literacy share mental processes that jointly support school readiness. Understanding these basic terms and ideas develops professional knowledge necessary for planning an effective preschool language and literacy curriculum.

> Defining key terms and explaining key concepts shows how oral language and preschool literacy share mental processes that jointly support school readiness.

Alphabet Knowledge

Alphabet knowledge is the ability to name and write the 26 alphabet letters. Alphabet letters are the building blocks of the English writing system. The name of an alphabet letter (e.g., *M*) often gives a clue to its sound, which is valuable information for emerging readers and writers. Children should know about 10 alphabet letters, including those in their own first name, before they enter kindergarten (U.S. Department of Health and Human Services, 2003).

Communication

Communication is the process of expressing and receiving ideas. It involves the exchange of meaning between people. Ideas can be sent and received in different ways, such as through gestures, pictures, and movements. Language is the richest and most versatile means of communication.

Communication Strategies

Communication strategies are ways to promote a rich exchange of ideas between or among individuals. Different from communication skills (e.g., controlling voice volume), strategies involve a plan of action for engaging others in meaningful exchanges. Effective communication strategies include asking and answering questions; clarifying and elaborating on topics; wondering aloud and commenting on the ideas of others.

Language

Language is a verbal system consisting of words and rules for organizing and changing words. The basic components of oral language are called phonemes—elementary units of sound that are combined in various sequences to form morphemes. A morpheme is the smallest sequence of phonemes that can carry a meaning that can be isolated in a sentence in any given language. By combining these phonemes and morphemes, we can construct as many words as we like. We can then combine these words with one another to produce a potentially infinite number of sentences. From birth, children are exposed to the language of their families; they learn the words their families use and develop their own grammar style to combine and change words. By age 4 most children have grasped the grammar rules of their language and increasingly use language for social exchanges, requests, finding out, telling, and play (see Table 1).

Literacy

Literacy is a written system of marks that fixes language in place so it can be preserved. It involves the reading, writing, and thinking needed to produce and comprehend texts. Spelling and punctuation rules govern our writing system and must be learned if one is to become literate. Depending on their family literacy environments, children begin forming ideas about books and print in infancy. By 2 years of age, they may pretend to read to dolls, stuffed animals, or themselves. And by age 4, many can read environmental print, their own name, and a few common words (e.g., *hello* or *exit*). In kindergarten, children start to read predictable books and spell

Table 1
Milestones in Language Development

Age	Language Milestone
3 months	Makes cooing sounds
11 months	Uses multiple-syllable babbling (*mama, dada, baba*)
16 months	Uses some words besides *mama* and *dada*
23 months	Can form two-word sentences
34 months	Uses prepositions; carries on a conversation
47 months	Can be understood by strangers most of the time

Note. Adapted from Vukelich, Christie, & Enz (2002).

Table 2
Early Stages of Reading Development

Stage	Reading Development
Stage 0: birth–age 6	• Grows in control of oral language • Relies heavily on pictures in text • Pretend reads • Hears sounds in words; recognizes rhyme
Stage 1: ages 6–7	• Aware of sound–letter relationships • Maps speech to print and sounds out words • Attempts to break code of print • Uses decoding to figure out words
Stage 2: ages 7–8	• Develops fluency • Recognizes patterns of words • Checks for meaning and sense • Knows a sight vocabulary

Note. From Chall (1983, 1996).

simple words. By age 8, most children are expected to read and write at a third-grade level (Snow et al., 1998). Table 2 provides an overview of the early stages of reading development.

Oral Language Comprehension

Oral language comprehension is the ability to listen and respond with understanding. To comprehend oral language, children need to pay attention and listen with purpose. They need to accurately and quickly recognize the words they hear. At the same time, they need to connect the new information they hear with what they already know. From this, children build meanings that indicate the comprehension of ideas, as shown by what they do and say. Children's oral language comprehension abilities improve when they are read to, asked interesting questions, given clear explanations, and encouraged to express their ideas. Reading aloud storybooks—conducting read-alouds—is especially beneficial, because while listening to stories and information books children also learn book language, book structure, new concepts, and new vocabulary. These opportunities not only build the skill of listening with understanding but also expand children's background knowledge and the amount of words they can use to talk about experiences.

> Oral language comprehension is the ability to listen and respond with understanding.

Oral Language Instruction

Oral language instruction is a learning context that can be used to purposefully teach children about language and how to effectively develop reading, writing, speaking, and listening skills. Much of children's oral language learning occurs through conversations with adults and peers, but not all. There are several effective instructional techniques that are geared to teaching oral language skills to the young child, such as storytelling.

Phonological Awareness

This involves hearing the sounds of language apart from its meaning. This mental work is difficult for most children. It requires them to become consciously aware of the structure of language, rather than simply using language to communicate. They need to learn how to listen with purpose for the number of words in sentences (e.g., *We / had / eggs / for / breakfast.*), the number of syllables in words (e.g., *fish-er-man*), and the number of individual sounds in words (e.g., /h/, /a/, /t/). Phonological awareness is a strong predictor of future reading success and an essential skill for phonics and spelling (Stanovich, 2000). The following vignette is an example of preschoolers demonstrating phonological awareness by manipulating the beginning sound to generate a rhyming word.

* * * * * * * * * * * * *

Adult: I'm thinking of a word that begins with /m/ and rhymes with *fan*.

Children: *Man!*

Adult: *Man*. That's right. When you put /m/ and /an/ together you get *man*.

Adult: Now I'm thinking of a word that begins with /s/ and rhymes with *bunny*.

Children: *Sunny!*

Adult: And what else?

Children: *Funny!*

* * * * * * * * * * * * *

Speech

Speech refers to the activities of articulating and uttering sounds to produce sequences of words. Barring hearing loss, all children gradually learn to use speech to express meaning as they talk. Speech develops in an orderly and predictable progression, from babble to single words to two- or three-word utterances and finally to complex sentences. The rate of development, however, varies tremendously in individual children. Some children are early talkers while others are late talkers. Put another way, some like to "schmooze," tending to be more social, while others are too busy or absorbed in activities to talk.

Substantive Conversation

Substantive conversation is a form of talk between adults and children that informs, explains, and elaborates on ideas. It often includes teachable moments, when adults have the opportunity to provide background knowledge on topics. It involves expanding the amount of child talk in a conversation and stretching the conversation to add details, new words, and new language structures, such as adjectives and adverbs, idioms, and figurative language.

Talk

Talk is the means through which children's use of language occurs. Through talk with others, children build their practical knowledge of language—the verbal system. They learn to talk by talking. This is how they learn new words and gain mastery of language rules. Children's language knowledge (words and rules), gained through talking, becomes the basis for developing essential reading and writing skills. How much and how well children can use language is evident in their talk, as in this account of young Lucy's tonsil operation.

• • • • • • • • • • • • •

Lucy:	I won't even feel anything when I got my tonsils out.
Adult:	You didn't feel anything?
Lucy:	I had some purple juice that made me asleep and I didn't even feel anything.
Adult:	Oh.
Lucy:	Had this big ange [bandage] here sticking on my arm. And they had to sew it together.
Adult:	You were brave.
Lucy:	Very brave! It didn't hurt—very much, no.

• • • • • • • • • • • • •

Vocabulary

Vocabulary is used to describe the store of words children know. It is organized into two large types: (1) expressive vocabulary, which are those words children can use to express themselves, and (2) receptive vocabulary, which are those words they can understand when heard in context. Generally children's receptive vocabulary (listening) is larger than their expressive vocabulary (speaking). The average preschooler knows about 5,000 words and by the end of high school will have an estimated vocabulary size of about 60,000 words (Bloom, 2000). Vocabulary is learned gradually over many encounters with a new word again and again (Stahl, 2003). Children benefit from language-rich environments that expose them to many new words used many different times in many different ways.

Three Fundamental Concepts

Before children are readers and writers, they are speakers and listeners. Progressing from saying words to reading and writing them demands an intellectual shift in children's thinking. They must become conceptually aware that there is a code to be deciphered and that it is different from speech. Reading print is more than understanding speech written down.

The following concepts explain how oral language and literacy are both alike and different. See Table 3 for an outline of Halliday's (1977) functions of language, and see Table 4 for five functions of early literacy (Neuman & Roskos, 1989). Note how the functions or uses of language and literacy overlap. Both, for example, are means for interacting with others. However, their uses also differ in important ways. Literacy, for example, is used for exploring the world through print (signs), whereas language is used to explore the world through oral exchanges. When you know more about the relationship between speech and print you can help young children make the mental shift from the more familiar world of talking to the less familiar one of reading and writing.

Concept 1: Talk and Print Are Alike

Talking, reading, and writing are interrelated processes. All three involve using words to *stand for* or represent persons, objects, and events in the world. Each draws from the other in real experience. Children speak and listen, they listen to reading, they read what they write, and so on. These overlapping processes are what Vygotsky (1962) described as "tools of the mind" that children can use to get things done. Talking, reading, and writing join together to build children's knowledge about the world and about

Table 3
Language Functions That Children Learn

Function	Example	Purpose
Instrumental	"I want"	To communicate desires, wishes
Regulatory	"Do as I say"	To control behaviors of others
Interactional	"Me and you"	To manage the social environment
Personal	"Here I come"	To express self, feelings
Heuristic	"Tell me why"	To ask about the world
Imaginative	"Let's pretend"	To create new worlds

Note. From Halliday (1977).

Table 4
Literacy Functions That Children Demonstrate

Function	Example	Purpose
Exploratory	"How does it work?"	To experiment with print
Interactional	"Between you and me"	To share information
Personal	"For me"	To claim ownership
Authenticating	"To legitimate"	To act grown up
Transactional	"Between me and text"	To label; to make meaning

Note. From Neuman & Roskos (1989).

words. At the starting line of learning to read and write, children rely on their considerable speech experiences to help them with print experiences.

Concept 2: Talk and Print Are Different

There are important differences between spoken and written language that make learning to read harder than learning to talk. Why? There are two main reasons. First, print is a code for speech that relies on the manipulation of a set of symbols (26 alphabet letters), and because it is a code, children need to be taught how to decode print before they can say it. This extra step requires extra mental effort. Adults must help children find the relationship between print symbols and speech sounds and help them make the effort to remember. Second, print is decontextualized: It does not have the real-time qualities of speech, such as tone, pitch, expression, and rhythm, that signal meaning. Before they go to school, children experience mostly talking that occurs in rich contexts. When a mother says to her 4-year-old son, "Put on your pajamas. It's time for bed," there are real environment cues to help him know what this means. Children also interact with peers in rich, meaningful, social play situations that provide many signals about what to say and do. Even speech on television and computer games has many sensory clues as to what the talk refers to and why a person is talking.

Print is different. It is silent and still. Its meaning must be unbundled from the print itself by an active mind. This, too, requires extra mental effort to pick out the meaning from the words alone. Adults must show children how to think with print to make it meaningful. This is why reading to and with children is so powerful—because it shows them how to do what they need to do to comprehend the print code.

Concept 3: Speaking, Listening, Reading, and Writing Share Skills

Fortunately, concepts and skills learned for oral language are shared with literacy and vice versa. A few of the most essential are making predictions, asking and answering questions, telling and retelling, sense of story, and phonological awareness. You can think of these skills as *crossover strategies* because they are used in children's talking, reading, and writing to the benefit of all three. Knowing about these strategies will help you be more effective and more efficient as you plan language experiences for the eager talkers and emerging readers and writers in your setting.

Making Predictions.   This is the ability to use context to choose the appropriate language. At a friend's birthday party, children remember to say "Happy Birthday" because the setting reminds them of the event. As a familiar bedtime favorite, they can chime in, chanting "Chicka, chicka, boom, boom" as you read aloud the storybook to them. Similarly, they use the skill of prediction to guess what a printed word might be when they hear its beginning sound or connect visual cues with the meaning (e.g., the tail-like form of the letter *g* at the end of the word *pig*).

Asking and Answering Questions.   In oral language, questions are signs of seeking, noticing, and incorporating new and more complex experiences into prior experiences. They signal what's going on in children's minds while mental schemas are being organized and built. Questions indicate children's skill in monitoring comprehension; through their questions, we can see that children are "following along" and "getting it," whether it be a conversation, a book reading, a play episode, or a table activity. Questioning is a vital skill in speaking and listening as well as in reading and writing.

Telling and Retelling.   These expressive verbal skills exercise children's use of language to tell, recount, report, explain, and pretend. Children need many opportunities to practice their expressive language skills so that they learn to include the details. In speaking, listening, reading, and writing, details matter. Attention to detail increases the length of sentences, the size of vocabulary, and the grammatical complexity of the talk. Details also enlarge the child's store of background knowledge.

Sense of Story.   Children's personal stories about their real experiences indicate their storytelling abilities. Stories are one way they learn to represent their experience. Stories provide an organizer for holding an experience in mind and replaying it at will. Storytelling is also the forerunner of grasping the story structures found in literature. Children's oral storytelling abilities lay the foundation for using story elements to comprehend stories in books.

Phonological Awareness.   As a skill, phonological awareness places special demands on children's abilities to self-regulate their thinking and actions. They must listen for specific words or sounds; listen to words and sounds carefully to manipulate them; and listen with the intention to act for a specific purpose, such as clapping for each word heard in a sentence, tapping for each sound heard in a word, completing a rhyme, singing and clapping in rhythm, and so on. Learning to read and write depends heavily on phonemic awareness, which is the basis of matching sounds to printed letters and decoding printed words.

Observe (or videotape) children conversing in a natural setting (e.g., eating, playing, waiting). Complete the following chart. What are concrete examples of each function? Are some functions used more often than others? Is there evidence of early literacy functions? You might find it interesting to compare the language of children of various ages. What are the differences between 3- and 4-year-olds, for example, in the ways they use language and early literacy for negotiating the environment?

Function	Example(s)
Exploratory	
Interactive	
Personal	
Authenticating	
Transactional	

CHAPTER 3

Planning for Talking, Reading, and Writing a Lot

Aquality early childhood program that joins oral language and early literacy does not just happen. It takes planning, action, good management, and attention to the continuous improvement of instruction. Planning includes assessment that provides a clear picture of children's speaking, listening, reading, and writing abilities and what they can accomplish in the short term and over the long term of your program. It uses best practices to ensure that children are engaged and learning. It involves the effective use of resources, including time, materials, and other adults, to create the optimal supportive learning environment. Planning is the cornerstone of intentional teaching that helps children make good progress.

Long-Term Planning

Long-term planning describes the learning goals for children's oral language over the entire time of your program. To plan effectively, you need to be familiar with content standards in language and literacy that define expectations for young children.

You may already be familiar with the early learning standards in your state and use them regularly. To learn more you can browse the online Standards Database provided through the National Institute for Early Education Research (NIEER). See nieer.org/standards and select Facts and Figures to locate the Standards Database. The Standards Database categorizes the descriptions of state early childhood education standards and presents them in a common format. It is easy to use and provides helpful information about the structure of content standards and also gives examples of standards from 22 states. A related document, *Child Outcome Standards in Pre-K Programs: What Are Standards? What Is Needed to Make Them Work?* by Bodrova, Leong, and Shore (2004), also provides valuable information about the history, policy, and the construction of early learning standards.

In a nutshell, content standards are valid statements of expectations in oral language and literacy that young children should achieve before kindergarten. For the English-language learners (ELLs) in your classroom, look carefully for information about how these standards should be applied to them.

Standards help us to come to consensus on what children should know and be able to do. We can all agree, for example, that children should use an increasingly complex and varied vocabulary across the preschool years (a standard commonly cited in early learning standards documents). This is, of course, an important oral language goal in long-term planning, but it is too general for guiding everyday instructional activities.

Most preschool standards include performance indicators that detail what children should know and be able to do by a certain point in time. Performance indicators describe key knowledge and skill elements of a standard. They can also serve as instructional objectives for short-term planning in the preschool language and literacy program.

Short-Term Planning

Short-term planning outlines the major activities you will implement to meet the long-range oral language learning goals that support children's developing oral language concepts and skills over time. Consider a weekly planner for this purpose. To be effective (and practical), a weekly planner should be clear and concise, including enough details so that someone else could follow it if necessary, and short enough to fit on one piece of paper.

Look at the weekly planner example shown in Figure 3. It summarizes the activities in a preschool classroom during one week in October. Note that the planner has a place to record the current theme or unit, as well as the one that went before and the one coming up. This can help you to make connections across the many weeks of instruction. It organizes the main activities for the week, and includes relevant assessment activities. It provides space for indicating which standards areas are emphasized and encourages a coding system for recording specific performance indicators that are addressed. A space to document home–school connections is also available.

Figure 3
Sample Weekly Planner

Unit 1: Here I Am (Harcourt Trophies Pre-K [2005])
Last Theme: Going to School
Current Theme/Topic: Families
Next Theme: My Home

Objectives: Trophies	Daily Schedule				
	Time	Activity	Grouping		
			Whole	Small Group	Center
1. Identify author and illustrator (LL III-2) 2. Respond orally to Big Book and read-aloud books (LL III-5, 6) 3. Develop family-related vocabulary; Big Book new words; read-aloud new words (LL II-1) 4. Communicate ideas through letter-writing LL VI-3 5. Identify letters *M*, *m*, and /m/ sound (LL I-6) 6. Use position words in retelling In Between (LL II-4)		Getting Ready: Arrival routines		X	
		Circle I: Calendar, Sharing, Singing	X	X	
		Shared Book Reading:	X		
		Day 1: Picture Walk My Mother Is Mine; teach 2 new words	X		
		Day 2: Predict/check; track print; teach 2 new words	X		
		Days 3–5: Find words that start with *M/m*; list new words			
		Center/Activity Time:		X	X
Assessment(s): • Friday 5-minute conference and CBM with children who need support • Anecdotal notes on language use in dramatic play		Read-Alouds: *In Between* *Word Play Time: The Color of Us*		X	X
Content Standards in This Theme: • Coded identifiers from Ohio Early Learning Content Standards (www.ode.state.oh.us) • LL: I-5; II-4; III-6; V-4; VI-3; IIX-3; X-2 • M: I-1; II-3; V-1 • SC: V-1,7 • SS: II-1; VII-3		Dramatic Play: Family Trip		X	X
		Writing: Family Trees		X	X
		Books: Make a book: family scrapbook		X	X
		Blocks: From school to home		X	X
Home–School: Favorite Family Story		Discovery: Family Graphs		X	X
		Art: Family Portraits		X	X
		Circle II: Singing; Shared Writing (family letter)	X		

Weekly plans should reflect your long-term plan. Activities you plan each week should support children's reaching established early learning standards in oral language skills. They should address objectives or performance indicators that are directly linked to expected outcomes. Your weekly plans should also guide your daily planning to ensure consistency in children's language and literacy experiences. When long- and short-term plans are consistent with one another, opportunity for children to integrate their developing language and literacy skills is greatly increased.

Using Assessment to Inform Planning

Assessment is an integral part of intentional teaching and the basis of continuous improvement. It is a data-gathering process with the primary aim of determining what children can and cannot yet do. This information informs your instructional planning—both long- and short-term planning—and program decision making. It helps you to intentionally build connections between oral language and early literacy experiences. It is useful to start thinking about assessment as a coordinated set of multiple measures and methods or an assessment system. We describe this concept further later in this chapter. For now, a few basic guidelines are helpful.

Assessment should occur regularly to determine children's needs, help you plan, and guide your instruction. Various assessment tools are available to screen, monitor, and evaluate children's learning progress in oral language and early literacy skills. You should become familiar with some of the more common assessment tools in each of these assessment categories and be prepared to discuss the results with others. Short descriptions of several popular preschool language and literacy assessments are provided in the "A" section of the Appendix.

An Assessment System

There's more to assessment than pre- and post-tests, informal observations, or periodic parent conferences. To truly inform oral language learning and instruction, assessment needs to be thought of as a system of measures that provides reliable, valid information about an individual child's language development and communication skills. An assessment system allows teachers to find out children's current levels of performance, to keep track of their progress, and to test the strength of the oral language

---

Figure 4
Assessment System

Accountability	**Screening**	**Instruction**
≪≪≪≪≪	●●●●●	≫≫≫≫≫
Looking back	*Looking at*	*Looking ahead*
(Evaluate)	*(What is)*	*(What can be)*

Coordinated set of multiple measures and methods

---

curriculum in the preschool program. An assessment system contains three kinds of measures: screening measures, progress-monitoring tools, and performance evaluations.

Figure 4 illustrates the important parts of an assessment system that combine to provide a more comprehensive view of children's language and literacy learning.

Screening

Set aside time during the first few weeks of your program to determine children's speaking and listening abilities, as well as their literacy skills. We suggest that you use a formal screening measure for this purpose along with informal observations of children as they work and play together. One example of a formal screening measure is the Teacher Rating of Oral Language and Literacy, or TROLL (see Dickinson, McCabe, & Sprague, 2003). The oral language portion of this tool addresses essential speaking and listening skills found in most sets of preschool standards. No formal training is required to use the TROLL measure. It requires only 5–10 minutes for each child. Meet with each child in a quiet place to conduct the screening.

At other times during the day, use an informal checklist like that in Figure 5 to document individual children's use of language and oral language skills. Plan to focus on three to five children each day over a

Figure 5
Oral Language Checklist

Child Observed: _____

Observer: _____

Key: (+) Consistently (✓) Sometimes (−) Not yet

Date	Observational Setting			Comments
	Large Group	Small Group	Individual	
Speaking				
Responds when spoken to				
Takes turns speaking				
Participates in group discussions				
Recalls and recites songs and fingerplays				
Speaks clearly				
Speaks in complete sentences				
Initiates conversations				
Asks questions				
Tells a personal story				
Uses appropriate sentence structure (word order, pronouns, verbs)				
Listening				
Listens to rhymes, songs, and stories with interest				
Listens to speaker in conversations				
Follows single-step direction				
Follows multiple-step directions				
Vocabulary				
Plays with words				
Links new words to what is already known about a topic				
Uses new words appropriately in conversation and discussion				

From *Doors to Discovery Assessment Handbook*. Copyright © 2002 Wright Group/McGraw-Hill. Reprinted with permission.

24

two-week period. Compare your informal observations with those of a more standardized screening instrument.

Using a dual approach that combines formal and informal screening measures provides multiple sources of information, and is well worth your time and effort. A solid baseline of information helps you to tailor your instruction to the full range of children's oral language abilities in your classroom.

Progress Monitoring

For continuous improvement, it is important to keep track of children's progress while they are in your program. This will allow you to determine if children are developing adequately or need more help to thrive. We recommend that you organize a set of short speaking and listening curriculum-based assessment items that are strong predictors of school readiness for the purpose of tracking children's progress (Ergul, Burstein, Bryan, & Christie, 2007). Your set of assessment activities should tap the critical areas of oral language comprehension, vocabulary, and phonological awareness.

Examples of assessment items in each of these areas are provided in Figure 6. Note that there are only a few items in each area and that they are grounded in the preschool language and literacy curriculum.

Establish a time each week to check on a small sample of children in your classroom. A sample might consist of (a) only those children who are at risk, (b) two to three children from each group of at-risk, typical, and advanced children in your classroom, or (c) the majority of children in your classroom. Your goal is to monitor children's progress so you can assess how well your language and literacy program is meeting their needs. When data show that some children are not making progress, then aspects of your oral language program need to be revised or changed.

Evaluation

Assessment includes evaluation. It is necessary to find out if your program is effective and children are achieving goals in language development that develop oral language abilities and support early literacy skills. This can be done in at least two ways. Your program may already use a commercial test to determine children's achievement in key areas of language and early literacy upon program completion. Examples of commercial tests include the Peabody Picture Vocabulary Test, the Assessment of Literacy and Language, and the Woodcock-Johnson III Test of Achievement.

Check for a good match between your program goals and what the test measures before making judgments about program effectiveness. If no

Figure 6
Sample Items for Weekly Progress Monitoring

Name _____   Date _____

Purpose: Track how well the child is learning the vocabulary words and letters in the early literacy program.

Show Me (Identification):

Place picture word cards in front of the child and say, "We are going to look at these pictures. Show me the _____."

SCORE:
1 Point = Correct answer or self-correction within approximately three seconds.
0 Point = Incorrect answer.
NA (**N**o **A**nswer) = Asked twice and no answer at the end of three seconds.

Tell Me (Production):

Place the picture word cards in front of the child and say, "We are going to look at these pictures. Tell me the name of the picture I point to." Point to each picture and say, "Tell the name of this?"

SCORE:
1 Point = Correct answer or self-correction within approximately three seconds.
0 Point = Incorrect answer.
NA (**N**o **A**nswer) = Asked twice and no answer at the end of three seconds.

Alliteration (Identification of initial sounds):

Use alliteration picture cards.
Say, "Here is a picture of a [picture name]. Now which one of these pictures starts with the same sound?" Name the top picture and then point to each picture in the bottom and say out loud.

SCORE:
1 Point for each correct answer or self-correction within approximately three seconds.
0 Point = Incorrect answer.
NA (**N**o **A**nswer) = Asked twice and no answer at the end of three seconds.
Sample responses are not scored.

Rhyming (Identification of ending sounds):

Use rhyming picture cards.
Say, "Here is a picture of a [picture name]. Now which one of these pictures sounds like [picture name]?" Name the top picture and then point to each picture in the bottom and say out loud.

SCORE:
1 Point for each correct answer or self-correction within approximately three seconds.
0 Point = Incorrect answer.
NA (**N**o **A**nswer) = Asked twice and no answer at the end of three seconds.
Sample responses are not scored.

end-of-program assessment is required in your setting, you can repeat the screening, using the formal tool along with your informal observations as backup, to make judgments about how well children are doing and overall program quality. Using either of these approaches, the results from assessment should be used to describe where children presently are in their skill development and to make improvements in your program. One of the most powerful uses of evaluation is to improve the quality of your program to ensure children's high achievement in the essential oral language skills related to school readiness.

Second-Language Development

If you have ELLs in your classroom, you should become familiar with the stages of second-language development that researchers have noted for these children. Your assessment of their progress will depend on your knowing what to expect. The next section offers you a brief overview of the stages of second language development.

Researchers have outlined the following sequence of second-language development of young children (Tabors, 2008). Of course, as with all developmental processes, there are variations in how children approach this process and how long it will take for them to go through these stages. But it is clearly important to have these stages in mind when assessing ELLs' language use in your classroom.

First, the child uses the home language. When everyone around the child is speaking a different language, there are only two options—(1) to speak the language they already know or (2) to stop speaking entirely. Many children, but not all, follow the first option for some period of time (Saville-Troike, 1987). This, of course, leads to increasing frustration, and eventually children give up trying to make others understand their language.

The second stage is the nonverbal period. After children abandon the attempt to communicate in their first language, they enter a period in which they do not talk at all. This can last for some time, or it can be a brief phase. Although they do not talk during this time, children attempt to communicate nonverbally to get help from adults or to obtain objects. Furthermore, this is a period during which children begin actively to "crack the code" of the second language. Saville-Troike (1987) noted that children will rehearse the target language by repeating what other speakers say in a low voice and by playing with the sounds of the new language.

The next stage occurs when the child is ready to go public with the new language. There are two characteristics to this speech—it is telegraphic and it involves the use of formulas. Telegraphic speech is common in early monolingual language development and involves the use of a few content words without function words or morphological markers. For example, a young child learning to speak English may say "put paper" to convey the meaning "I want to put the paper on the table."

Formulaic speech refers to the use of unanalyzed chunks of words or routine phrases that are repetitions of what the child hears. Children use such prefabricated chunks long before they have any understanding of what they mean (Wong Fillmore, 1979).

Eventually, the child reaches the stage of productive language use. At this point the child is able to go beyond short telegraphic utterances and memorized chunks. Initially, children may form new utterances by using formulaic patterns such as "I wanna" with names for objects. In time, the child begins to demonstrate an understanding of the syntactic system of the language. Children gradually un-package their formulas and apply newly acquired grammar rules to develop productive control over the language.

Developing a Long-Term Plan: Learning Trajectories

Assessment informs instructional planning. Using assessment information and early learning standards, you are equipped to develop a long-term plan that addresses oral language development of the diverse learners in your classroom. In this effort learning trajectories can be useful guideposts. They can help you chart children's skill development in the five main areas of language we described in Chapter 1:

1. Semantics
2. Syntax
3. Morphology
4. Phonology
5. Pragmatics

From research we can derive realistic expectations of what children should accomplish as language users across the preschool years. Expectations can be plotted along trajectories or developmental paths that show what we should expect of children as they grow older. Preschool learning trajectories for oral language comprehension, vocabulary, grammar, and phonological awareness are illustrated in Figure 7.

Figure 7
Learning Trajectories

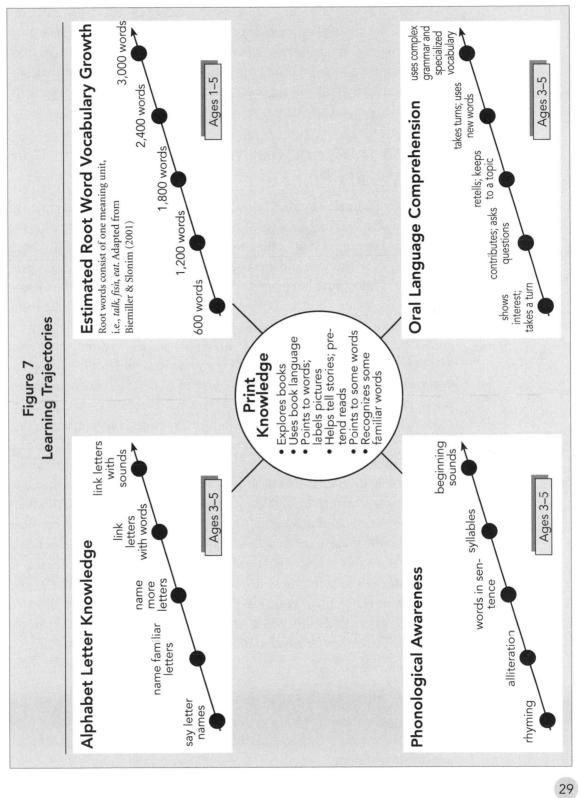

Estimated Root Word Vocabulary Growth

Root words consist of one meaning unit,
i.e., *talk, fish, eat.* Adapted from
Biemiller & Slonim (2001)

600 words
1,200 words
1,800 words
2,400 words
3,000 words

Ages 1–5

Alphabet Letter Knowledge

say letter names
name familiar letters
name more letters
link letters with words
link letters with sounds

Ages 3–5

Print Knowledge

- Explores books
- Uses book language
- Points to words; labels pictures
- Helps tell stories; pretend reads
- Points to some words
- Recognizes some familiar words

Oral Language Comprehension

shows interest; takes a turn
contributes; asks questions
retells; keeps to a topic
takes turns; uses new words
uses complex grammar and specialized vocabulary

Ages 3–5

Phonological Awareness

rhyming
alliteration
words in sentence
syllables
beginning sounds

Ages 3–5

In developing your long-range plan, you should use research-based learning trajectories to help you make decisions about the long-range goals of your program. You need to compare what children can do, gathered from your assessments, to benchmarks on the learning trajectories and plan language experiences that will support children's oral language development.

Putting the Long-Term Plan Into Action: The Weekly Planner

The weekly planner is a practical tool that serves as a bridge between the long-term plan and daily lessons. The planner helps preschool teachers to coordinate learning activities on a weekly basis so that they join children's developing oral language and preschool literacy skills. The day-to-day purpose is to connect oral language and early literacy learning to the advantage of both. When children improve their oral language comprehension, the foundation for later reading comprehension is laid. When they are guided to attend to specific sounds in language, children become better listeners who can get the most out of conversations and book reading experiences. As they interact with different texts, children encounter new words that increase the vocabulary they can bring to reading and writing.

When you make your weekly plan, you need to consider which oral language skills will be carefully guided and which ones will be less catered to in the round of daily activities for that week. You should think about what you will teach to the whole group of children, to small groups, and to individuals and ensure that children have ample time to explore new language uses, words, and print skills on their own. And you need to consider the instructional approaches you will use to expose children to thematic content that builds their background knowledge. For rich language use to occur, you need to bring these important considerations to mind as you prepare your plan for the week. A reproducible weekly planner is provided in the "C" section of the My ABCs Appendix, and you may find the sample planner in Figure 3 to be a useful model for your own weekly planning.

Routine Flow of Events

While organizing your weekly planner you may want to think about how oral language and early literacy skills can become well integrated into the routine flow of events.

Table 5
Sign-In Procedure

1. Prepare a sign-in sheet with the names of four or five children on each page.
2. Tell the children, "I need your help to keep daily attendance. Every day when you arrive, you will sign in. You will put your name on this sign-in sheet. Here's what you do. Find your name on the sign-in sheet. Write your name in the box next to it as best as you can. This is your signature. When you sign in, we all know you are here with us today."
3. Show the children how to follow the steps: arrive, go to the sign-in spot, find your name on the sheet, sign in.
4. Maintain the sign-in sheets in a folder to note children's progress in name writing.

Note. Adapted from McGee & Richgels (2003).

Greeting Time.   In addition to modeling and exchanging social courtesies that encourage speaking and listening, greeting time is an ideal opportunity for children to link language and literacy. One good idea is to have children "sign in" by writing their first names (or making their mark) on chart paper at an easel. See Table 5 for a sign-in procedure that requires children to write their first names as a daily attendance activity, which helps the children learn the alphabet letters in their own name.

Activity Time.   Much of activity time (play and table work) should be filled with language as children play together and work on small projects with adults. These are opportune times for conversation, discussion, and role-play. You should also deliberately use these times for modeling how to ask questions to clarify or gain information or analyze and explore ideas, and to prompt children to find solutions to questions such as, Why do our shadows become longer or shorter? What does the architect do? For ELLs you may want to model how children can ask for help from others (e.g., "Say to Sammy, 'May I have some play dough?'").

Circle Time.   Beyond shared reading and sharing time, consider using circle time or when you gather as a whole group for developing children's storytelling abilities and listening comprehension. Tell stories to children drawn from your own childhood memories. Assist children in having ideas about stories they can tell. Help them prepare. Invite them to share their own stories with the group. A storytelling program gives children practice in speaking in front of an audience, develops their sense of story, exercises their use of decontextualized speech, and is personally meaningful for them. These activities may be particularly challenging for ELLs. Make sure that they are ready to participate actively in these events. If they are not ready, find another activity that they can be part of that will let them show off their growing language competence.

Outdoor Time. Use outdoor time for extending language and literacy experiences by modeling new games children can play and for assisting children in using language effectively to negotiate the rules and procedures for play and to resolve conflicts. On neighborhood outings with the children, point out environmental print that is present on stores and businesses, posters and storefront advertisements, traffic signs, and so on. Carry information gathered on these walks back to your settings, incorporating it into your instruction and play areas.

Essentials in the Daily Plan

Your daily plan is your guide to action in the busy, unpredictable world of your classroom. It helps you to organize and manage your time with children to their benefit as learners. Time well spent involves you in working with the whole group, working with small groups, and having children play well independently.

When working with the whole group you should include some direct teaching and demonstrating of effective speaking and listening skills. For example, you might role-play language and appropriate behavior for buying or selling in the class Grocery Store. Plan to spend about 10–15 minutes each day teaching specific concepts and skills for talking, reading, and writing with a whole group of preschoolers. You should group children in pairs or small groups (three or four children) for instructional purposes. Children make better progress in these situations because they have more chances to use and attend to language under the guidance of an adult.

There are two different types of groups that work well—heterogeneous groups and homogeneous groups. Heterogeneous groups are made up of children with different ability levels; homogeneous groups gather together children with similar strengths and weaknesses. Neither type of group should be seen as permanent but rather as flexible, with children leaving and joining different groups depending on the instructional purpose. For example, you might gather one or two small heterogeneous groups together to make a sand clock in the whole-class exploration of time and timekeepers. Later, homogeneous groups of children may be formed for board games and puzzles that develop alphabet letter knowledge. This allows you to pitch your instruction so that it is neither too hard nor too easy for any one child in the group.

If you have ELLs in your classroom, consider how you can alternate their experiences, sometimes having them work with children who are more fluent in English and sometimes having them work in groups with other ELLs, so that you can tailor instruction to their needs.

One major concern for preschool teachers is what the rest of the children will be doing that is productive for them when you are working with small groups or pairs. So what should they be doing? They should be playing with one another in inviting, language and print-rich settings that advance their talk, reading, and writing. For this, you need to make sure that play settings stimulate pretending, content-oriented themes, and complex roles. You need to allow sufficient time for uninterrupted play, at least 45–60 minutes daily (Johnson, Christie, & Wardle, 2005). And you need to prepare children for play by helping them make a plan for their play, periodically checking in on their progress, and coaching them on the spot when they need help.

Set up your small-group work to allow time before and after to assist play activity. Play influences children's thought and language significantly (Smith, 2007). It allows children to think and do with language and literacy at a higher level than when in a real situation. It prepares them for abstract ideas and thinking that further oral language comprehension. Because play requires children to conform to roles and rules, it helps them practice self-regulation in thinking and actions (Diamond, Barnett, Thomas, & Munro, 2007). For these reasons, you need to be planful and purposeful in helping children play so as to better their talking, reading, and writing. Table 6 describes the characteristics of mature play that should be present by the end of kindergarten.

Themes

Themes organize language and literacy experiences around a robust set of ideas that are valuable to explore for both adults and children. Themes also facilitate the complex job of developing a long-term plan by providing manageable sets of ideas. Preschool teachers have long organized young children's learning experiences around themes or units. But, to deeply develop language and literacy skills for all children, not just any theme will do. You need to select themes that deliberately build children's world and word knowledge (Hirsch, 2003). Not only ordinary themes, such as "All About Me" or "Our Furry Friends," but also extraordinary, robust themes,

Table 6
Characteristics of Mature Play

Characteristic	Example
Symbolic representations and symbolic actions	"Would you come with us? Let's go to Sea World."
Complex interwoven themes	"We're following the treasure map to the scary mountain."
Complex interwoven roles	"You can be the customers and I'm the cash register guy. Jared's the waiter guy. OK?"
Extended time frame (over several days)	After two days: "We're still playing hospital and the babies got so-o-o sick."

Note. Adapted from Bodrova & Leong (2007).

Table 7
Features of a Compelling Theme

- Content rich: Children will gain world knowledge.
- Engaging: Children will find the topic interesting.
- Enduring: Children will remember important ideas and facts.
- Thoughtful: Children will learn to think and question.

such as "Fossils," "Gardens and Gardening," or "Color and Light," that introduce children to the powerful ideas of science, mathematics, social studies, art, and literature are needed. (See Table 7 for four features of a robust theme.) Such themes go beyond day-to-day knowledge and language to include rare vocabulary (not just everyday words) and all kinds of book language from stories to informational texts. When carefully selected and sequenced, themes provide cumulative and repeated opportunities to develop children's oral language comprehension, vocabulary, and print awareness.

ELLs also can benefit from these themes in the classroom. But it will be important to remember to present information in visual as well as verbal formats so ELLs can understand the topic of discussion. Presenting vocabulary with both visual and verbal cues will help all the children start to understand and use their new words.

Guidelines for Work and Play

For any place to run smoothly, it is necessary to establish rules, appropriate ways of interacting, and acceptable work. Children need to know what is expected of them. It is a good idea to post a daily schedule that shows the flow of the day. The schedule helps everyone to remember what comes next and also provides a written record of what has been accomplished.

Discussion of the daily schedule can become part of the everyday routine and at the same time draw children's attention to print and its uses. ELLs will find this routine extremely helpful as it will make the daily flow of activities predictable, enabling them to show that they know what is going on in the classroom.

Another useful tool is a play area board for organizing and managing children's play time. Figure 8 shows an example board that uses colors to represent five basic play areas: Library (Reading) and Writing—Green, Discovery—Purple, Blocks—Orange, Art—Red, Dramatic Play—Blue. Heavy chart paper holds the colored clips for each play area. Children

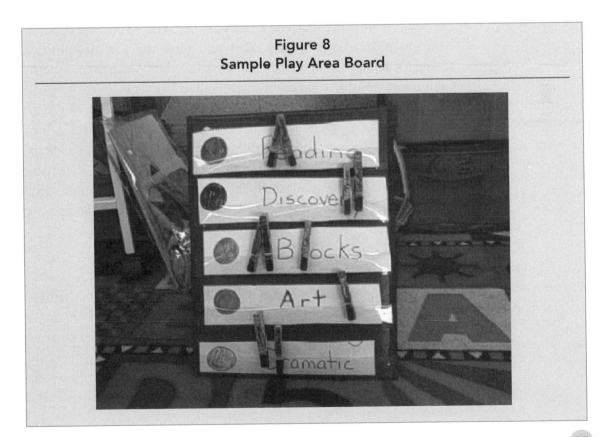

Figure 8
Sample Play Area Board

choose and take the clip or a similar reminder (e.g., a badge) to the play area.

You will need to teach the children how to use the play board, which will require several weeks of practice. But this is time well spent because it reduces interruptions while you are with small groups and it encourages children to take charge of their own play activity. Use of the board also benefits children's print awareness because they quickly learn to recognize their own as well as their classmates' names as play areas are selected. Some soon learn to read the names for the different play areas.

For children to work independently at an activity they need to know the rules that apply and the consequences of not abiding by the rules. You should ask the children to help you make the rules for work and play. One way to begin is to ask the children why it is necessary to have rules. Make a list of their responses on chart paper. Ask them what would be good rules for playtime activities. List these as well. Usually children come up with negative statements, such as "No hitting." When all the children have had a chance to contribute, ask them to help you group like rules into categories: For example, No hitting, No punching, Don't throw books, Don't spit on books, Don't leave things out, and Don't yell at each other. Ask the children to help you make a label for each group and guide them toward positive statements such as Treat others kindly, Work together, Make room for others, Put things away, Use materials carefully, and Use quiet voices.

Post the rules where children can easily see them, and refer to them when introducing new activities. If you consistently refer to the rules from the beginning of the year, children will soon learn what is expected of them in work and play activities. If you find that there are ELLs who are having difficulty with the rules, it may be that there is miscommunication about what is expected. Working directly with parents on these issues and asking parents to explain the rules to their children may help the situation.

Making the Most of Resources

Every early childhood setting contains resources in terms of time, people and materials. Your careful use of these resources can maximize children's language and literacy experiences to the fullest. You need to set up your daily schedule with an emphasis on children's active learning with you and their peers in uninterrupted time blocks. Snack time, for example, is an informal time for talking, just as nap time is a stretch of time for listening to stories and pretending to read all by oneself.

Adults are one of the richest resources for children because they can bring considerable knowledge, language, and print to them. One effective way to involve adults is to have them participate in topics or themes you are exploring with the children. For example, when Ben Mardell's preschoolers studied squirrels, he invited Judy Chupasko from the Mammalian Department at Harvard University's Museum of Comparative Zoology to his class (see Mardell, 1999). Judy explained the preparation of animals used in scientific study, which fascinated the children and also introduced them to the idea of anatomy—mapping the insides of things.

Teacher assistants are an excellent resource in supporting the language and literacy curriculum. They can assist with progress monitoring and other assessment activities. They should be actively involved in your read-aloud program, reading at least two or three books per day to small groups of children or individual children. And they should be richly supporting children's project activities and dramatic play. Working as a team, you and your teaching assistant greatly increase the learning potential of the preschool environment.

Involve parent volunteers meaningfully in the day-to-day. They can join children at play on a regular basis. In this informal setting they can watch and learn, they can take roles and participate, or they can show children how to play a game. Adult presence is encouraging to children and stimulates them to play for longer periods of time. When adults join in they engage children in conversation, they use new words and more complex sentences that enrich children's speaking and listening (Neuman & Roskos, 1993).

For second-language learners, make time to bring their home languages into your classroom. Often, teaching assistants are fluent in a language other than English and can read a familiar book to the whole class in that language. Or parents can come into the class to read in their home language. The children whose home language is being used will be thrilled, and the other children will get to hear the sounds and vocabulary of another language.

Materials are the stock-in-trade of a well-provisioned early learning environment. Along with everyday supplies such as writing tools, equipment, and charts, they include the books, toys, software, eBooks, and websites that widen the world of preschoolers. Materials should be of high quality to engage preschoolers' active minds as well as their active bodies. And they should represent the cultural diversity of the children in the classroom. The Evaluation Checklists for Books, Toys, Websites, and

Software located in the "C" section of the Appendix provides a good start for choosing high-quality materials that meet your oral language instructional goals.

Early childhood settings where children talk, read, and write a lot are the result of planning. When you make the effort to coordinate expectations, assessment information, learning activities, and curricular resources in long- and short-term plans, you go a long way toward ensuring a high-quality language learning environment for all the young children in your program.

FOR FURTHER EXPLORATION

Go to the Appendix of this book and look at the assessments listed. Try to obtain one and administer it to a preschool child. Based on the results, what long- and short-term plans would you make for the child? Refer to early learning standards, developmental milestones, and learning trajectories in your planning.

CHAPTER 4

Creating a Supportive Learning Environment for Child Talk

Children thrive in learning environments that help them to use what they already know to make sense of new information, to build an understanding of facts and ideas, and to check that their own thinking and actions are in line with the goals of an activity. Creating a supportive learning environment where young children can work, play, and learn with understanding and joy is the *sine qua non* of effective preschool practice. It is absolutely essential for ensuring children's oral language development and for establishing a permanent connection between oral language abilities and emerging early literacy skills. Children succeed when they are provided with learning conditions that nurture their language discoveries, their different uses of language, and their first attempts to read and write. When you create a supportive learning environment for talk you also create opportunities for children to learn together about the real world and about possible worlds; where they can discover the uses of their minds, imagination, materials, and new technologies; and where they can feel a part of a friendly (and smart) community.

Of course, supportive learning environments are created through different styles and approaches, but all reflect three important elements: good conversation, effective conversational strategies, and interesting instructional activities. In this chapter, we briefly highlight key features of these design elements that when sensitively combined create enriching oral language environments where children's talk (and laughter) abound.

Substantive Conversation

Substantive conversation is a form of talk adults can use to engage children in long and rich dialogues about important topics. The need for such conversation between adults and children and among children is very great, driven by a basic human need to know; to tell; and to explain about yourself, your experiences and the world around you. How can teachers routinely stimulate substantive talk with the children in their preschool classrooms? Rich talk and compelling themes are two top-notch ways to encourage substantive talk more often in the classroom setting. Opportunities for rich, extended dialogues on content-rich topics build up children's expressive and receptive vocabularies—and vocabulary acquisition is at the heart of language development.

Rich Talk

One way to ensure a lot of substantive conversation is to stimulate talk that is rich with ideas, facts, observations, connections, and feelings that relate to children's immediate experiences. This is often easier said than done in the preschool classroom. Managing groups of young children in classroom space can preclude long and rich dialogues in quiet, intimate places where conversations can go on at length. Recall all those "one shots," or short exchanges, about clean-up, wash-up, and line-up that so often occur in the course of the preschool day.

Yet despite these realities, rich talk can be supported in different activities that make up the preschooler's day. Children are more likely to engage in rich talk, for example, when engaged in familiar routines and activities. Familiarity with what they are doing frees them to give their attention to talking about what they are doing—in other words, they are able to use language over action. Therefore, routine activities are fertile ground for engendering rich talk between children. This is illustrated in the following conversation between Kathy and Tylea (4-year-olds), who are drawing bugs on (and in) the ground around a tall tree on a mural-in-progress about spring. Notice how they use language to talk about language—in this case, writing the word *ant* on the mural. They name animals and insects—*butterfly, snail, spider*—and they use descriptive language, like *crawley*.

• • • • • • • • • • • • • • •

The teacher helps the girls get started, saying, "Maybe the ants go down here in the soil." She points to the area beneath the tree. Kathy is drawing a snail while Tylea sketches ants.

Kathy: I can write *ant* by that…there you go. I did it for you.

Tylea: What's your next writing?

Kathy: I don't know. Another ant. I'll write that here. I can do it.

Tylea:	I'm gonna make my ant blue. I'm gonna make a butterfly behind the snail.
Kathy:	Look! I found the snail in the bug book. Do you like my snail? Isn't it cute? Now next is gonna be a spider. Spiders come out, too.
Tylea:	Eeeek! I don't like spiders. They're crawley. I already drawed one down here.

• • • • • • • • • • • • • • •

Rich talk is also more likely to occur in dramatic play. This activity presses children to use language to imagine, to negotiate roles, to describe actions, and to explain the rules of play. For example, in the following play scenario, several children are running a flower shop and negotiate their roles in the shop.

• • • • • • • • • • • • • • •

The play starts with a short disagreement about whether the shop is open or closed, but the children eventually decide that it's open. The following takes place between two boys.

Boy 1:	Okay. It's open. Order something. Some prette-e-e-e flowers.
Boy 2:	I don't wanna be the person buying flowers all the time.
Boy 1:	Okay, fine. You can be the cash register guy—over here. [motions behind the counter]
Boy 2:	Then you can buy the roses, the daisies, and stuff. Okay?
Boy 1:	I'd like to place an order for flowers, please.
Boy 2:	Okay what do you want? The roses? The daisies? These pretty purple ones here?
Boy 1:	I wanna buy some flowers for my wife. Here's the money. She's over there.
Boy 2:	[to his assistant] All right, we need flowers for the wife. Make it roses...the redder ones.
Boy 1:	Thanks. Keep the change.

• • • • • • • • • • • • • • •

Small-group activities and one-to-one interactions between adults and children offer many opportunities for rich talk. This is especially so when the activities have a clear goal and adult talk is contingent on the child's talk, as in the following conversation about a pleated skirt between Eugenia and her father. Note how the child asks, the exchange persists, and the adult and child work together to come to a satisfactory answer.

• • • • • • • • • • • • • • •

Eugenia: Daddy, what's a pleat?

Dad: A pleat? I've never heard of a "pleat." What do you think it is?

Eugenia: A skirt?

Dad: Oh, I think you mean a pleated skirt...someone talked about a pleated skirt.

Eugenia: Yeah—she was wearing a pleated skirt.

Dad: Do you remember when you spin around and have on a pleated skirt, and the skirt rises up? The pleats are folds of cloth and when you spin around they spread apart. Do you remember?

Eugenia: Yup.

Dad: That's what it means—pleats. The pleats—the folds—of the skirt spread apart.

Eugenia: Oh, I get it.

• • • • • • • • • • • • • • •

Compelling Themes

Another means of bringing about substantive conversation in your preschool classroom is the deliberate use of compelling themes. We touched on this traditional practice in the previous chapter, but expand on it a bit more here because of its high relevance in creating a supportive learning environment specifically for child talk.

A theme-based approach is certainly not new to early childhood education, but our intentions can be fresh and new. A 21st-century goal is to use themes that strengthen and build children's word and world knowledge. For this we need compelling themes that organize experiences, activities, projects, and play around strong early learning standards in language arts, mathematics, science, social studies, the creative arts, and health.

You might be wondering what an example of a compelling theme is. An exemplary illustration of the use of a compelling theme can be found in Ben Mardell's preschool classroom during their Squirrel Unit (Mardell, 1999).

• • • • • • • • • • • • •

Step inside Ben's preschool classroom. Hear the excitement as the children get ready to become Squirrel Scientists for the next four weeks. Today the children are getting ready to go on a daily walk around the neighborhood to create their Squirrel Census. Their goal? Count all the squirrels they can spot.

On the walk they talk about squirrels and Ben talks to them about different colors of squirrels as well as their habits. Another day the children and their teacher gather in a classroom "squirrel lab" to think about what squirrels eat. Aviva wonders if squirrels eat snakes, but Shoshanna and Jessie vehemently disagree!

Ben also introduces the class to a scientific drawing of a squirrel with labels. He asks the children to make their own observational drawings and learn about the heart, the lungs, the stomach, and of course the bushy tail.

Across the four weeks these students read squirrel stories, draw and write squirrel books and silly squirrel stories, and even watch a real squirrel scientist, Judy, from the Natural History Museum as she shows the internal anatomy of a squirrel specimen. Ben's preschool squirrel scientists have become squirrel experts in this compelling theme that includes science, the environment, problem solving and reflection, writing, reading, and even number sense. Who wouldn't want to be a scientist after exploring this theme?

• • • • • • • • • • • • •

Four features of the Squirrel Unit transform it from an ordinary learning experience to a robust one that develops content knowledge, therefore making it a compelling theme.

1. *It is content-rich*: It incorporates concepts, facts, and skills from a variety of content areas. It addresses a full range of early learning standards and provides many varied opportunities for learning, especially in science.

2. *It is engaging*: This theme interests and excites these children, who are tremendously curious about their world and knowledge seekers about living things in their immediate surroundings.

3. *It is enduring*: Through its activities, projects, and play, children are exposed to powerful disciplinary ideas that they can remember and use later on in future learning, such as keen observation, careful drawing, and accurate labeling.

4. *It is thoughtful*: The theme challenges children's thinking and stretches their skills to new levels. It supports intellectual achievement.

Effective Conversational Strategies

Good conversation, they say, is an art. It is especially the case when adults seek to have substantive conversations with young children. Fred Rogers, host of the well-known educational program *Mr. Rogers' Neighborhood*, as we know, was a master at conversing with young children, inviting them to talk along and listen with comprehension. Few are as accomplished as Mr. Rogers in the fine art of conversation with preschoolers, yet there is also a science to having good conversations with young children that teachers can learn. From research we know of several effective talk strategies that can make the difference between many good conversations between teachers and children, and not having so many.

The following sections explore three conversation strategies that should be a part of every preschool teacher's communication skills repertoire: (1) Clarify—Extend, (2) Question—Tell, and (3) Think-Aloud. We provide further information about interaction frameworks and language scaffolds in the "C" portion of the Appendix.

Clarify—Extend

Research tells us that when adults define words, when they disentangle confusing ideas and terms, and when they add details to conversations, children learn more language and are exposed to more new words (Bloom, 2002). Here's how it works:

- Listen to what a child says.
- Pick up on an idea from the child's talk.
- Add to it, explain it further, and disentangle any confusions.

The following example illustrates how an adult clarified and extended what his daughter said.

* * * * * * * * * * * * *

Heather: Are those the trees that they're talking about?

Father: Yeah, those are pine trees.

Heather: We have pine trees out back.

Father: We have some, but not so many, do we?

Heather: Yeah.

Father: Remember there were so many in Maine. Sometimes when the fog came up we couldn't see them, remember that? Real gray and foggy. Then when the fog went away we saw all little islands filled with trees just like that.

* * * * * * * * * * * * *

Question—Tell

Research supports asking questions and telling answers as effective ways to interact with young children so long as these talk strategies are contingent or built upon the child's interests and efforts (Wood, McMahon, & Cranstoun, 1980). Here's how it works:

- Join the child in an activity.
- Draw attention to parts and details.
- Maintain interest with talk contingent on the child's effort.
- Offer praise and encouragement.

Consider the following example in which the teacher helps Simon complete a puzzle (Wood et al., 1980).

* * * * * * * * * * * *

Simon: Are there pieces missing here?

Teacher: You'll have to start the right way up. You have to get them all turned over the right way.

Stephanie: Can I do this?

Teacher: You can do that one, Stephanie, yes. I put this out for a little girl.

Stephanie: I'm a big girl.

Teacher: Oh! You are a big girl. I'm sorry.

Simon: Does this go at the top?

Teacher: Yes, Simon. Look at the top of that clock again and that's the one that comes right at the very top. Look the big hand's on it. Can you see? Right, start off with that, all right?

Simon: This at the top.

Teacher: No, that one comes next, doesn't it?

Simon: Then...then that one goes in there and the one goes there!

Teacher: That's right. Now you've got the idea.

Simon: That goes there.

Teacher: Good boy.

Simon: I am doing very much.

Teacher: You're doing very much. That must be because you're 4 now, right?

Simon: Yes.

• • • • • • • • • • • • • • •

Stephanie, as you will likely have observed, does not need any help because she is a "big girl." Note, too, the contingent uses of language by the teacher. She *tells* relevant information in response to the children's questions. She *asks* leading questions, such as "Right, start off with that, all right?" And she provides immediate feedback: "No, that one comes next, doesn't it?"

Think-Aloud

A think-aloud is just that: A time when adults say what they are thinking as they do something or consider a problem. Adults instill a sense of inquiry in children when they frequently show their own thinking and wonder about things around them. When they model curiosity and think aloud, they expose children to the abstract uses of language, such as imagining, and demonstrate an attitude of learning (Tough, 1981). Here's how it works:

- Involve the child in what you are doing.
- Verbalize your thoughts.
- Model how to think through a task or problem to a conclusion.

Consider the following example. Pay attention to how the teacher talks about what she is thinking, as in, "You know, I can observe this apple with all my senses." She then continues to "think aloud" as she describes the attributes of the apple.

• • • • • • • • • • • • • •

Ms. Marci is using circle time to introduce the children to the vocabulary and methods of *observe*, *predict*, *check* in science. She shows them an apple and says, "You know I can *observe* this apple with all my five senses. I can see that it is red. I can feel that is smooth on the surface. It's not a cold thing and it's not a hot thing. I can shake it, but it does not make a sound—none at all. But, you know what? I cannot see inside the apple right now. So I can only *predict* what is inside— maybe white stuff and seeds. How can I *check* that out, I wonder?" She then asks the children how they might check out her predictions.

• • • • • • • • • • • • •

Effective Instructional Techniques

Much of children's oral language learning occurs through conversations with adults and peers—but not all. To master the less obvious oral language skills that are the foundation of literacy, children need to be given oral language instruction. They need to be taught, for example, to pay attention to how words rhyme, to manipulate morphemes (e.g., plurals), and to listen for main ideas. They need guidance in what to say and when in social situations. At times, preschool instruction in oral language skills should be direct and explicit. But at the same time interactions need to be sensitive, responsive, and playful. This is no easy feat! Fortunately there are several instructional techniques that are geared to teaching oral language skills to the young child.

The Dialogic Reading Technique

Dialogic reading is a conversation between an adult and children about a book. To have a substantive conversation that extends children's use of language, you need to apply a set of prompts. You can remember these prompts with the acronym CROWD (Bowman, Donovan, & Burns, 2001).

C   *Completion prompts*: Leave a blank at the end of a sentence for children to fill in. For example, "Jack and Jill went up the hill to fetch a pail of _____." This prompt exercises children's sensitivity to the structure of language.

R   *Recall prompts*: These prompts encourage children to remember what happened in the book. For example, you say, "The little red hen wanted to make some bread. Do you remember what happened when she asked for some help?" Use this prompt to help children organize the story and remember its sequence.

O   *Open-ended prompts*: These prompts focus on the pictures in books. You might say, "It's your turn to read the story. What is happening on this page?" When you encourage children to help tell the story, you provide practice in expressive fluency and attention to detail in illustrations.

W   *What, where, when, and why prompts*: These questions also focus on the pictures in books. When you ask, "What's this?" you are teaching children new words. When you ask, "Why do you think the puppy is sad?" you are encouraging them to retrieve words from their own vocabulary store to express their opinions.

D   *Distancing prompts*: These prompts guide children to make connections between the book and their experience. For example, reading *Brown Bear, Brown Bear, What Do You See?* (Martin, 1996), you ask, "Do you have goldfish at your house? Does your goldfish have a name?" Distancing allows children to practice their conversational and storytelling skills.

The Language Experience Approach

The Language Experience Approach (LEA) is a longtime favorite of both adults and children. It involves child dictation of a common experience with the adult as the scribe. For example, the following experience was dictated by three boys about their Block Area play experience while the teacher recorded their dictation.

This is an aircraft carrier. We took four of these big things and a helicopter and one of these little things and a motorized van and we put them all together. The helicopter and the motor cycle battled. Chucky, Jason, and of course me, Jeremy, made it.

Language experience dictation holds a wealth of opportunity for children to use language and to see literacy in action modeled by the adult. Even better, it results in a written text that children can revisit often to remember and try reading on their own. The basic procedure for LEA is outlined in Table 8.

Table 8
Language Experience Approach

Step	Explanation
Step 1: Have a common experience	Share a common experience with children, such as a nature walk, field trip, guest presentation, or special event.
Step 2: Take dictation	Ask the children to help you remember the event by writing about it. Have them recall highlights and write their comments on chart paper. Read back each child's contribution, pointing to the printed words. Talk about what the words look like and how they sound. Compliment the children on their word choices.
Step 3: Read the story	Once you have a complete story that captures the common experience (about four or five sentences), read the text to the children. Then read it again and invite the children to read along with you as you reread the piece. Finally, read it one more time. This time, pause to let individual children "read" portions of the story.
Step 4: Explore the story	Now have some fun with the story. Engage children in discovering letters ("Let's find all the M's in this story and circle them with a red marker.") or words ("Let's look for that word *geranium*. Remember we saw those beautiful red flowers on our walk."). Help them search and find specific alphabet letters and words. Help them listen for sounds in key words.
Step 5: Read the story again	Post the story on an easel for reading again at a later time. At each return to the story, make instructional points related to oral language comprehension, vocabulary, phonological awareness, and alphabet letters. Provide copies for children to "read" on their own and to take home.

Sing, Say, Read, and Write Pocket Charts

Songs, rhymes, and poems are an ever-fresh source of delight for young children. These playful ways with words improve children's memory, phonological awareness, vocabulary, and creative uses of language. On occasion you should capture the spirit of songs, rhymes, and poems by writing them down and displaying them in pocket charts for children to sing, say, read, and write on their own. Here's what to do over time:

1. Choose a song verse, chant, nursery rhyme, or short poem.

2. Sing, chant, or say the selection with children. Have them repeat phrases to help them learn the piece.

3. Write the words on sentence strips in front of the children. Say each word as you write the phrases and sentences. Then sing, chant, or say each phrase or sentence as the children watch. Invite them to chime in. Place the strip in the pocket chart. When the entire selection is placed in the chart, sing, chant, or say it through in its entirety while pointing to the words.

4. Have the children close their eyes and mix up the sentence strips. After they open their eyes have them help you put the strips back in order.

Wall Calendar for Daily News

A wall calendar is a good way to enrich your setting with print and provide opportunities for children to talk, read, and write on topics of special interest to them. It also offers a refreshing alternative to the traditional calendar approach because it include the Daily News and increases the number of children who can participate in calendar activities. Follow these steps:

1. Select a wall space for the calendar. You will need enough space to display five 8 ½ × 11-inch sheets of manila paper one for each day of the week.

2. During Calendar Time, have an 8 ½ × 11-inch sheet of paper ready on a nearby easel.

3. Following your calendar routine, work with the children to record the following information on the manila paper: day of the week, date, weather, and one newsworthy item (e.g., "We are going to the bakery today."). Write the text in large print.

4. Ask for a volunteer or two who will make a drawing for the calendar page at the art table. Talk about what the drawing might be and what colors to use. Be sure to make a note of who is illustrating the page for the day.

5. Collect the calendar page at the end of the day. Consider any other additions, such as photos or three-dimensional items that might increase interest and add visual detail. Attach the page to the wall or a wire in sequence as the days of the week pass.

6. Each day, review the Calendar Wall with the children. Help them remember past events and recall details for each day. Have them practice remembering the names of the days of the week and counting.

7. Repeat steps 1–6 for each week of the month. If possible, display each week, moving each passing week further up the wall to create a giant calendar of the month. Put a pointer by the calendar so that children can locate specific days and view, read, and remember events that have passed.

8. When the month has passed, assemble the pages into a book. Make a cover (e.g., *The Merry Month of May*). Put it in the library center for children to look at and read on their own.

Plan for Play

Play is most beneficial for learning when it involves pretending and creating a play story that lasts for an extended period of time. You can enrich the learning power of play when you help children plan for it (Bodrova & Leong, 2007; Soderman, Gregory, & O'Neill, 1999). Follow this procedure for play planning:

1. Provide background knowledge for a new play idea by reading to children or going on a field trip.

2. Ask the children to help you change a play setting for the new play theme.

3. On chart paper, print the name of the play theme (e.g., The Kids' Café).

4. Ask children to tell you things that this play setting will need to work. Write down their ideas. Remind children to listen carefully. Someone else may have thought of their idea already. If so,

children can put up a thumb so that others know they had that idea too. (You may end here for the day or continue.)

5. Ask the children to suggest where the class might get these items. Note the source next to the items on the list (e.g., Miss Carol's house, Tanya's house, the center, a store).

6. Have the children help you decide how to get the supplies—ask for donations, bring them in from home, etc. Make decisions about who will bring in the supplies.

7. As the supplies come in, check them off the list. This can be done at the start of play time or during group time. Have the children help you compose and mail thank-you notes to those who contributed.

8. Meanwhile, ask the children, "What roles do we need for this play idea?" List the roles with a job description for each (e.g., Waiter: takes orders, delivers food, tells the cook what to make).

9. With the children's help, set up the play setting during play time or tell them you will be setting it up and to look for it the next day.

10. As the play begins, move it along by asking questions, such as "How will I know the Café is open?" to motivate reading and writing or by taking a role to model the use of language and introduce new words.

What About English-Language Learners?

Several of these instructional techniques are already popular in the preschool setting and used routinely. Will you need to change the way you think about creating a supportive learning environment for talking, reading, and writing for your ELLs? The answer is not at all. However, at first, you will likely need to do more of the talking. But don't be discouraged that an English learner does not respond right away to your attempts at conversation. Remember that there is likely to be a nonverbal period for ELLs when they will be trying to make sense of the new language that is being used in the classroom. During that time they will be getting used to the new sounds of the language and will be beginning to try to understand what different words mean. They will not start using their new language until they feel comfortable that they have something to say and they know the right way to say it. And even after they begin to use their new language, there will be a lot that they won't know how to say.

By carefully setting up everyday conversations, guided participation, and language scaffolds, you will be helping the ELLs as well as the other children in your classroom. So even if the ELLs aren't using their new language yet, they are developing important information. And when they do start to use their new language all of these techniques will help them to learn more quickly.

FOR FURTHER EXPLORATION

Like the language-friendly classroom, the home environment needs to be language-rich, too. Write a newsletter (e-mail, brochure, PowerPoint for parent's night, etc.) for parents and caregivers that explains the three design elements discussed in this chapter (time for conversation, conversational strategies, instructional activities) and the key features of each tailored to the home environment. Be sure to include clear, relevant explanations that parents and caregivers will understand. Use examples so they can easily see how to promote high-quality language experiences in the home.

CHAPTER 5

Using Best Practices to Join Oral Language and Early Literacy Learning

Best practices describe the routine use of instructional approaches and techniques that help children learn well. Best practices come from evidence in the research as well as the professional wisdom of the early childhood field. In language and preschool literacy professional literature, there is consensus around five best practices (Dickinson & Neuman, 2006; Ehri & Roberts, 2006; New Standards Speaking and Listening Committee, 2001; Roskos & Christie, 2007; Wells, 1986). They are as follows:

1. Shared book reading

2. Songs, rhymes, and word play

3. Storytelling

4. Circle time

5. Dramatic play

In this chapter, we describe five best practices that provide instructional frameworks for effective language and literacy instruction in the early years. We delve into these best practices as a means of joining oral language and early literacy learning in early childhood settings. These five practices make sense today based on what we know; however, we need to be mindful that early childhood education research is ongoing, as is our own practical experience, and thus our best practices of today are evolving and should remain open to revision and change for tomorrow.

Our descriptions include instructional frameworks (organizers for instruction), protocols (blueprints for teaching actions), sample lesson plans, and connections to standards. These are the teachers' tools for designing effective preschool literacy instruction. In addition, we articulate what has come to be known as the before-during-after (BDA) instructional framework, which organizes the key phases of instruction in classrooms. In the "Before" phase, teachers prepare children for learning by building on their prior knowledge. Throughout the "During" phase, they monitor children's oral language comprehension and early literacy skills. In the "After" phase, they help children make connections and consolidate their learning—until the next time. Each of the best practice classroom examples is situated within the BDA structure as a generic framework for effective instruction.

Shared Book Reading

Shared book reading is the cornerstone of a well-integrated language and preschool literacy program. Founded on the traditional bedtime story routine, where adult and child share the warm intimacy of reading together, shared book reading is a rich context for lots of talking and print referencing (Holdaway, 1979; Kaderavek & Justice, 2002).

In the early childhood setting, a Big Book or other enlarged text is often used to share a story with the whole class or a small group of children. The Big Book allows all the children to participate actively in the reading of the story. If there are ELLs in the class, keep in mind that a shorter reading session or one that is tailored specifically for them may work best.

> Instruction that occurs through shared book reading helps children develop oral language comprehension and print knowledge.

Instruction that occurs through shared book reading helps children develop oral language comprehension and print knowledge. They learn new words. They learn the basic skills of book handling, such as orienting from front to back and left to right, page turning, and distinguishing print from picture. They begin to follow along a line of print and start to identify predictable words and phrases.

Instructional Framework

The instructional framework of shared book reading is based on what is often referred to as gradual release model. The pattern is something like this: "First, I'll tell or read the story. Then we will tell or read it together. Finally you can tell or read it on your own." Through repeated readings, the responsibility for telling or reading the story is gradually released from the adult to the child. During this process the teacher provides considerable instruction to support listening comprehension skills, vocabulary development, sound awareness, and print concepts.

Teaching Protocol

Table 9 outlines a three- to five-day teaching protocol frequently used in shared book reading. First, look at Day 1 of the protocol and the multiple opportunities to develop children's oral language as they talk about the upcoming story. They hear language and use language as the stage is set for learning in the context of a book.

Table 9
Teaching Protocol for Shared Book Reading

Day 1

Phase	(Teachers) Teach	(Children) Learn
B	Tell title, author, illustrator	Attend to words; literary terms
B	Discuss cover	Make predictions
D	Picture walk	Comprehend oral language
D	Teach vocabulary *optional*	Say new words
A	Connect to experience	Remember; make connections

Day 2

Phase	Teach	Learn
B	Read title, author, illustrator words	Attend to print; literacy content
B	Read predictions *recorded from day before*	Print helps us remember
B	Recall new words	Remember new words
D	Prepare for reading	L-R orientation; print is read
D	Read; discuss	Comprehend story meaning
D	Teach two new words	Learn two new words
A	Confirm predictions	Check predictions
A	Connect to experience	Make connections

Days 3–5

Phase	Teach	Learn
B	Ask to read title, author, illustrator	Read words
B	Recall story events	Sequence of events
D	Ask to help read; use cloze	Track print; read words
A	Teach rhyming words	Hear rhyme
A	Teach beginning sounds	Sound–symbol matching
A	Hunt for letter names	Recognize letters
A	Predict word from 1st letter	Predict words

Note. B = before reading, D = during reading, A = after reading.

Next, look at Day 2 of the protocol. Note how oral language and early literacy intersect at this point in the shared book reading routine. During this second reading children are guided to connect the language they use with written language and print vocabulary.

Finally, the teacher can return to the book one or more times to help children make more connections between their oral language and printed text. Note that in the protocol for Days 3–5 the increasing emphasis on joining specific oral language skills, such as phonological awareness, sound–symbol matching, and story retelling, to the literary genre of narrative and a focus on words.

A few other considerations to bear in mind include book selection for shared book reading and pacing. Texts with cumulative, repetitive, or patterned texts are often more successful because they allow children to participate in the experience by repeating patterned lines and predicting story development. Maintaining a brisk pace of instruction before, during, and after a session is also essential to keep children engaged. Before-reading activities should spark children's curiosity, during-reading activities should contain lively conversations, and after-reading activities should motivate children to learn more about content and the book. Once the class is finished with the book, place the book conspicuously in the classroom library and encourage children to make return visits to the book for projects, play, and browsing.

Teaching Vocabulary During Shared Book Reading

> Even the single reading of a storybook can have an impact on children's vocabulary learning.

Research tells us that shared book reading provides an opportunity to teach children new words (Robbins & Ehri, 1994; Sénéchal, 1997). Even the single reading of a storybook can have an impact on children's vocabulary learning (Sénéchal & Cornell, 1993). Therefore, in the following section, we share a few techniques that guide vocabulary instruction in shared book reading. Here are three you may find helpful in your own practice.

Say-Tell-Do-Play.   The Say-Tell-Do-Play technique (Roskos, 2008) is easily inserted into the shared book reading routine, but it does call for teaching more than a couple of words on Days 1 or 2. Select five words to teach that the children probably do not know and that they need for school learning. A good source for these words is included in the "C" section of the Appendix.

Table 10
Say-Tell-Do-Play Protocol

Book	SAY	TELL (Definition)	DO (Action)	PLAY
The Ear Book (Perkins, 1968)	clock	used to tell time	Point to a clock	The telephone game where a message is sent from child to child
	flute	a musical instrument that we blow in to.	Use fingers to pretend playing a flute	
	snore	to make a loud noise from your nose when you are sleeping.	Make snoring sounds	
	slam	Slam means to bang/shut something really hard.	Close book with force	
	drum	A drum is a musical instrument that we beat on.	Use hands to pretend playing a drum	

Before you read, present each word to the children with an accompanying prop or picture. Say the word, then have the children say the word. Tell the meaning of the word (using a child-friendly definition), and then ask children to turn and tell a friend what the word means. During the reading, stop when you encounter each new word. Briefly tell what the word means and have children turn and tell a friend again. Use a gesture or action to add to word meaning. After the reading is completed, play a short game or role play with the children to encourage them to use the new words. Review the example provided in Table 10.

Tier 2 Word Technique. Using a BDA approach, the Tier 2 Word Technique (Beck, McKeown, & Kucan, 2002) is used after a text is read. Select two or three new words that are (a) important and useful for children to know, (b) instructionally powerful for making connections to other words and ideas, and (c) knowledge-builders in that they expand word meanings, such as multiple meanings, figurative speech, and so on. The following steps outline how to use the Tier 2 Word Technique:

Step 1: Remind children of how the word was used in the story.

Step 2: Ask them to repeat the word so that they create a sound impression of the word in their minds.

Step 3: Explain the meaning of the word in child-friendly language.

Step 4: Provide examples in sentences different from the story.

Step 5: Ask children to provide their own phrases or sentences with your support.

Step 6: Ask them to say the word again to establish phonological awareness of it.

Step 7: Repeat the above steps for each new word.

Step 8: End by using all the new words together.

Although it seems like a lot, the routine moves quickly once put in place. An example of the technique in action is provided in the upcoming lesson plan using *The Little Red Hen* (Ottolenghi, 2001).

SEER.   This instructional protocol for vocabulary, developed in the Phoenix Early Reading First Program by Shelley Gray of Arizona State University, is a four-step routine that contains many of the same elements as Say-Tell-Do-Play and the Tier 2 Word Technique. Its brevity makes it easy to remember and to "slip into" a shared book reading or read-aloud situation. Here's how it works:

S Say the word in a context that sheds light on its meaning (photo; sentence; props).

E Explain the word using a child-friendly definition.

E Exemplify the word by giving an example from your own or the children's experience.

R Repeat the word by asking the children to say the word after you.

An Authentic Shared Book Reading Lesson— The Little Red Hen

Shared book reading provides instruction that helps children to use their minds well in a meaningful context. In this respect, it is authentic instruction because it helps children to construct knowledge, to use essential language and literacy skills, and to engage in meaningful activity (Newmann, 1998). *The Little Red Hen* lesson in Figure 9 illustrates a typical shared book reading routine not uncommon in today's preschools. Pay close attention to

---

Figure 9
Shared Book Reading Lesson Plan for *The Little Red Hen*

Book: *The Little Red Hen*
Objectives:
- Understand the meaning of new words *[V1]
- Recognize predictable patterns *[RA-L5]
- Hear syllable segments in words *[PA2]
- Clearly express ideas *[C4]

Day 1   B: Show cover; read title; identify author and illustrator
               D: Take a picture walk; develop story line
               A: Recall earlier story *Rosie's Walk;* discuss ideas

Day 2   B: Ask children to read title; clap syllables heard in each word
               D: Make and record predictions at stop points; discuss ideas
               A: Teach the words *thresh* and *husks*. Use Tier 2 Technique.

Day 3–4   B: Recall author; discuss related books; reread predictions
               D: Use cloze technique to predict words; clap syllables for target words
               A: Teach the words *wheat* and *grind*. Use Tier 2 Technique

Day 5   Make bread!

Tier 2 Technique in Action:
1. In our story, the little red hen threshed the wheat so she could make bread. Do you remember what she did when she threshed the wheat?
2. Say the word with me: *threshed*. When something is threshed it means to get the grain (the seeds) out of their dry shells or their husks by hitting them. Wheat is threshed in the late summer. We say the farmers threshed the wheat. They use big machines, called combines, to thresh the wheat.
3. What else do you think farmers thresh on their farms? I am thinking of something horses like to eat. (Farmers thresh oats.) I am thinking of some seeds that birds like to eat. (Farmers thresh sunflower seeds.)
4. Say the word threshed with me again: *threshed*. We can also say *thresh* and *threshing*. Right?
   [Repeat the above steps for the word *husks*.]
5. We talked about two new words: *threshed* and *husks*. *Threshed* and *husks* are words we use to talk about harvesting wheat to make bread. The little red hen cut the wheat and threshed it to get the grain out of the stiff husks. She's a busy hen!

Note. Early Learning Standard Identifier taken from *Early Learning Content Standards*, Ohio Department of Education (2004). See www.ode.state.oh.us. B = before reading, D = during reading, A = after reading.

its underlying "Read To," "Read With," and "Read by Yourself" structure. As described previously, the teacher initially *reads to* children, then encourages children to *read with* the teacher as they enjoy the story, and then finally to have student try to *read by yourself* in repeated readings of the story.

Standards Connection

Shared book reading is a best practice replete with opportunities to address early learning content standards in the oral language domain. From a New Standards perspective (New Standards Speaking and Listening Committee, 2001), it supports instruction that develops children's speaking and listening skills in three key areas. The practice cultivates certain habits or dispositions necessary for social and academic experiences, such as conversing at length on a topic and discussing books. It engages children in narrative and informational text genres as kinds of talk for sharing knowledge and expressing ideas. It strengthens language use and language awareness of words and phrases. Children practice the rules of interaction, learn new words, and increasingly become aware of sounds in words. Most important, however, regular use of shared book reading nurtures a love of books and language—two strong foundations for school readiness.

Songs, Rhymes, and Word Play

Research clearly shows that the origins of phonological awareness are found in the singing, rhyming, and word play that all young children so enjoy (Adams, 1990; Burgess, 2006; Goswami, 2001). For the young child, the pleasure is in the rhythmic singing and saying that can involve the whole body in swinging and swaying. For the teacher, songs, rhymes, and word play activities provide teachable moments for "tuning" the child's ear to sounds in the speech stream. And this fine-tuning in the auditory channel is the foundation of phonological awareness in the human brain—that bridge from oral language to literacy (Wagner & Torgeson, 1987; Wolf, 1991). Understood in this deep sense, the teaching of songs, rhymes and word play is serious business indeed.

Coincident with children's delight in songs, rhymes and word play is the vigorous exercise of paying attention to similarities and differences in how words sound, what words mean, and how to pronounce them. Who has not heard a son, daughter, nephew, niece, or little neighbor struggle to say such words as *spaghetti, teeth, grandmother*, and so on.

It is especially noteworthy that the predictable patterns found in many songs, rhymes, chants, and finger plays help children develop sensitivity not only to beginning sounds, but also to ending sounds that are alike (e.g., "Ding dong, bell/Pussy's in the well/Who put her in?/Little Tommy Green/ Who pulled her out?/Big Johnny Stout"). Hearing similar ending sounds as well as beginning sounds (alliteration) is an essential building block in constructing a concept of the word in print—the very idea that spoken language can be represented in another way (Morris, 1992).

Perhaps not surprising, singing songs and saying rhymes are activities that help ELLs use their new language orally for the first time. The elements of playing with sounds, group recitation, and movement all seem to make it easier for ELLs to participate in activities and "go public"— sometimes as loudly as possible.

Instructional Framework

Yes, there is a framework that supports instruction in songs, rhymes, and word play, although such teaching may seem intuitive for many. Recall, however, your educational goal: to promote phonological awareness and language awareness in young children. To this purpose, the instructional framework is intentional and includes these basic parts: introduction, practice, extension, and review (Adams, Foorman, Lundberg, & Beeler, 1998).

More memorable, perhaps, is to think of the framework in these terms: Say/Sing, Recite, Invite, Replay. First, you introduce the song, poem, or word play activity (e.g., sound manipulation, nonsense words, made-up songs) by singing, saying, or playing it. Next, you recite or say the lines, the lyrics, and the word play sounds/words so children can attend to the words. Then you invite children to join with you in reciting the song, rhyme, or word play. Finally, you replay the song, rhyme, or word play game many times so that children can remember the piece in part or in whole. Sounds easy enough for lots of singing, chanting, rhyming, and playing with sounds and words on a regular basis, don't you agree?

Teaching Protocol

Table 11 shows what the teacher should be doing (intentionally) so that children can be cultivating their sound awareness of words and sounds in the speech stream through songs, rhymes, poems, and word play. The table describes the instructional framework over a period of three to five days, although phonological and language awareness activities often occur over shorter periods of time. On Day 1, note the emphasis on familiarizing the children with the *whole* song, poem, or word play, and attempts to tune their ears to the sounds and rhythm of the oral language.

Observe that on Day 2 the emphasis shifts to helping the children learn the song, poem, or word play by drawing their attention to the words

Table 11
Teaching Protocol for Songs, Rhymes, and Word Play

Day 1

Phase	Teach	Learn
B	Tell title of song, poem, word play	Attend to words; literary terms
B	Show props or related objects	Attend to words; literary terms
B	Sing, say, play activity	Comprehend oral language
D	Invite to join in	Say new words
D	Connect to experience	Remember; make connections

Day 2

Phase	Teach	Learn
B	Post written copy; read title	Attend to print; literacy content
B	Recite song, poem, word play	Listening skills
B	Point to words rhyming, unconventional, alliteration	Listen for and identify sounds
D	Recite and children echo	Say words with prosody
D	Gestures; actions	Listening and moving, e.g., clapping
D	Teach new words	Learn new words
A	Sing, say, play activity	Hear sounds in language
A	Connect to experience	Enjoyment with language

Days 3–5

Phase	Teach	Learn
B	Ask to read title	Read words
B	Ask to help recite	Recognize words
D	Sing, say, play	New song, rhyme, word play
A	Teach rhyming words	Hear rhyme
A	Teach beginning sounds	Hear beginning sounds
A	Play with sounds	Oral blending
A	Play with unconventional uses of words	Word meanings

Note. B = before reading, D = during reading, A = after reading.

and their features. The teacher points out words that rhyme or that are unusual, and adds gesture to help children remember the different words and phrases. She helps them to practice coordinating words and actions to remember the song, poem, or word play. By the end of the Day 2 they can sing, say, play with assistance—and begin to enjoy their language use.

When the children are familiar with the song, poem or word play, the teacher can then draw their attention to the details of sounds and words—how they are alike and different, and to other imaginative uses. Two items are noteworthy at this point in the protocol: Increasing children's sound and language awareness, and encouraging a sense of fun and play. In the end, we want children to know *and* love the songs, poems, and word play we introduce them to so that they sing, rhyme, and play with words on their own (and with gusto!).

Song, rhymes, and word play are not strangers to the language and literacy curriculum, and bring much joy into the preschool day. Their significant roles in developing children's phonological awareness is more recent, however. When teachers use these activities intentionally, they develop children's phonological and language awareness. They teach them the rhyming, alliteration, and segmentation skills they will need for later reading and writing.

An Authentic Song Lesson—"Old MacDonald"

We have tried to make the point that songs, rhymes, and word play are excellent (and fun) activities for systematically teaching oral language skills that are foundational in learning to read and write. This is a relatively recent idea based on a considerable amount of current early literacy research. But let's see how it works with an old song, one that has delighted every young preschooler every time it is sung: "Old MacDonald" (see Figure 10).

Standards Connection

Teaching songs, rhymes, and word play is a best practice that links most closely to phonological awareness. Using these activities, the teacher can provide instruction that develops the listening comprehension and oral blending skills that are the forerunners of literacy. End-of-preschool standards set an expectation that most preschoolers should recognize and produce rhyming words, identify words that begin with the same sound, segment words into syllables, and rapidly name pictures of common objects. They should readily participate in word play and show imaginative uses of language in reciting songs and poems. To meet these expectations, teachers need to plan for and expertly use songs, rhymes, and word play in their daily instruction—they need to routinely implement this best practice.

Figure 10
Lesson Plan for Song Using "Old MacDonald"

Song: "Old MacDonald Had a Farm"
Objectives:
- Differentiate between sounds that are same/different *[PA3]
- Name items in common categories *[V3]
- Participate in a song recitation and extensions *[C7]

Day 1	B: Introduce the song; link to current theme; use animal props
	D: Sing song with enthusiasm and gusto
	A: Ask children to tell favorite animal and the sound it makes
Day 2	B: Post written copy; recite (say) song verses
	D: Ask children to say verses with you
	A: Invite children to sing song with you more than once
Day 3–4	B: Invite children to recite (say) verses with you
	D: Associate sound with animal; initial phoneme play with animal name *a cow says coo-coo-coo-c[k]ei-c[kei]-o*; Farm Animal Sort: Wild/Domestic
	A: Sing song; add movement
Day 5	Sing song with puppets; post song in Library Area for reciting

* Early Learning Standard Identifier
Note. B = before reading, D = during reading, A = after reading.

Storytelling

Storytelling is a very old, time-honored form of instruction used by all cultures to teach children about their immediate environment and the wider world. It is also one of the earliest expressions of the language arts to appear in children. Every child has a story to tell and seeks an audience for it, even if the audience is composed of sleepy dogs and mute dolls.

As a best practice, storytelling is a valuable medium for developing the oral language skills of active listening and oral expression. To understand a storyteller, children need to be active listeners—predicting, checking, and integrating what they hear into a comprehensible story. To be storytellers, they must use their expressive vocabulary, narrative skills, and sense of audience to tell a good story.

When you implement this best practice, bring storytellers from different cultures into the classroom. If these storytellers can tell tales in the

> As a best practice, storytelling is a valuable medium for developing the oral language skills of active listening and oral expression.

home languages of your ELLs, they will provide those children with a sense of pride in their home languages and will provide the English-speaking children with the understanding that storytelling is a part of many cultural traditions.

Instructional Framework

The instructional framework of storytelling is a three-part structure that (1) models storytelling for children, (2) guides the development of story-telling skills, and (3) supports children as storytellers. This model–guide–support framework can be implemented over the entire program year as an integral part of your language and literacy program.

Storytelling on your part begins with the selection of several good stories to tell over time. You will use these storytelling events as a way to model storytelling skills for your children. Some helpful guidelines (Breneman & Breneman, 1983) for selecting stories are as follows:

- The story is age-level appropriate with easily understood words.
- The plot has action and creates a stage for what is to come.
- The story uses repetition, rhyme, or silly words.
- The values and models presented are appropriate for today's children.
- The characters are memorable.
- Taste, smell, sight, sound, and tactile descriptions create richness and depth.
- The story line is strong, clear, and logical.
- The storyteller likes the story and is eager to share it.

Once you have made your selections, you are ready to use the teaching protocol outlined in the next section.

Let's pause, though, for a few pointers on how to model good story-telling skills. For any story you choose to tell, thoroughly know it in your own mind. You might want to create a cue card for yourself to help you remember relevant details. Consider using props, such as flannel board figures, objects, pictures, or on-the-spot sketches. Emphasize repetitive phrases so children can join in. Vary your tone, speed, volume, and pitch to pique and sustain interest. And, of course (like any good performer), rehearse the story several times before orally telling it.

Once you have modeled a few good stories, help children start to tell their own stories and begin to build up their storytelling skills. At first, you may need to provide them with storytelling ideas and topics, such as a retelling of a well-known fairy tale or relating a personal experience. Show them a few basic storytelling strategies, such as using props, varying your voice, and rehearsing the story out loud. Confer with your new storytellers to prepare a storytelling session. At the session, provide assistance only if necessary, allowing the novice storyteller to carry the responsibility for relating the tale and connecting with the audience. Conducted regularly and in a sensitive, supportive manner, storytelling exercises a full complement of oral language skills, including the following:

- Demonstrating language cohesion (logical, sequenced retells)
- Using tone, volume, pace, intonation, and gesture to enhance meaning
- Taking into account audience and purpose when speaking
- Using vocabulary
- Practicing models of correct English

Teaching Protocol

Because storytelling skills encompass so many dimensions of oral language, they are developed gradually across the program year. The protocol provided in Table 12 outlines the key steps that support teaching and learning in implementing storytelling as a best practice. Note that this protocol does not reflect a BDA approach but rather follows the structure of the gradual release instructional framework. Storytelling abilities are built from strong, clear models of storytelling. Observe the high points of the storytelling modeling phase where language use strategies are clearly demonstrated (e.g., using props).

The guide segment of this best practice helps the teacher make that important transition from modeling storytelling to showing children how to tell a good story. Note the emphasis on using language for social interaction (e.g., considering your audience) and language for thinking (e.g., planning for the storytelling session).

The final segment in applying this best practice is the most fun. It is "show time" when the well-prepared, young storyteller takes center stage and tells the tale while the supportive teacher remains backstage offering prompts and gentle reminders as needed. The preschooler audience gets a chance to practice their best listening comprehension skills, and when all

Table 12
Teaching Protocol for Storytelling

Model Storytelling Skills

Teach	Learn
Model the language and structure of a story	Sense of story; vocabulary; models of English
Use props to highlight setting, characters, and story events	Story elements; language cohesion
Use voice to enliven setting, characters, and story events	Listening comprehension skills (e.g., paying attention); variations in language use
Attend to audience and purpose; encourages participation	Using language to communicate ideas to others

Guide Storytelling Skills

Teach	Learn
Provide ideas or topics for stories	Stories have a purpose; a point
Suggest props; ask leading questions about setting, character, and plot	Logical, sequenced retells
How to prepare for storytelling *individual conference*	Planning; using tone, volume, pace, intonation pattern and gesture to enhance meaning
Rehearsal	Using language for a specific purpose

Support Storytelling Skills

Teach	Learn
Demonstrate good listening skills	Active, attentive listening
Positive attitude toward the storyteller	Audience participation; response
Encourage the storyteller	Language to suit different purposes

is said and done, it is their appreciative claps that reward and motivate the budding storyteller.

At this point you may be thinking that there is more to storytelling as a best practice than you once thought. To have an impact on children's oral language communication and comprehension requires considerable long-range planning across the program year, not to mention the thoughtful, regular inclusion of storytelling in your themes and units. Yet for children to truly "take on" the storytelling skills that you model, deliberate attention

---
Figure 11
Lesson Plan for Storytelling Using "The Gingerbread Man"

Story for Telling: "The Gingerbread Man"

Objectives:
- Attend to speakers, stories, poems, and songs *[C1]
- Understand the meaning of new words *[V1]
- Identify characters in favorite books and stories *[RA(L) 1]

Day 1	B: Introduce the folk tale to the class; link to current theme
	D: Tell story with props *rolling pin, spatula, cookie cutter*
	A: Ask children to repeat *Run, run as fast as you can. You can't catch me—I'm the Gingerbread man!*
Day 2	B: Ask children to repeat the refrain and to say it when you pause
	D: Tell the story with the props; encourage the children to participate by saying the refrain
	A: Ask children to tell/recount their favorite part
Day 3–4	B: Ask children to tell the setting, character, and plot
	D: Tell the story using flannel board props; invite the children to help you as needed
	A: Use a story drama technique to have children retell the story
Day 5	Put flannel board and props in the Art/Drama Area; encourage the children to retell the story using the props

---
Note. Story drama is the re-enactment of a story by the children as it is read by the teacher. See full description in the "C" section of the Appendix. B = before reading, D = during reading, A = after reading.

needs to be paid to preparing them and supporting them in their own storytelling. What this might look like is illustrated in the sample lesson in Figure 11.

An Authentic Storytelling Lesson— "The Gingerbread Man"

"The Gingerbread Man" is a wonderful tale to share as a storytelling lesson. The focus of this lesson is on modeling storytelling skills that in later lessons the children will be guided to use in their own retellings of this tale. At the lesson level, we can see more clearly the BDA approach that organizes the teaching of storytelling strategies and skills. Note how each day of this lesson for developing children's storytelling skills includes a "Before" phase to prepare for learning, a "During" phase to develop skills, and an "After" phase to reinforce the development of skills.

Standards Connection

Storytelling links to content standards in two key oral language learning areas: narrative and creative arts. As a genre, storytelling teaches children how to create their own narratives in chronological order and how to orient their listeners by giving information as to the who, what, when, and where of the experience. As a production, it teaches them how to attend to a performance (the storytelling event), react to it, question it, and imitate it as a form of public speaking. Thus, in several important ways, storytelling is a best practice rich with potential for meeting expectations of speaking and listening in the preschool years. From a New Standards perspective, for example, the practice offers opportunities to address many of the oral language skills discussed in Standard 2: Kinds of Talk and Resulting Genres, including producing narratives as a genre, and producing and responding to performances, such as storytelling and read-alouds (New Standards Speaking and Listening Committee, 2001).

Circle Time

Every preschool classroom has its circle time when the teacher gathers the children around to discuss the order of the day and other relevant matters. In fact, a kind of circle time happens in some shape or form in nearly every classroom when prior events are recalled, news is shared, and an agenda for the day is set. Too often taken for granted, circle time is an essential practice in developing language skills for social interaction. It is in circle time, where children become aware of social conventions, such as listening to others and conversational turn-taking. They learn the rules of polite discussion and how to explain ideas and experiences to a group. They use the words and terms of daily life in a literate society—the days of the week, the weather, newsworthy events, a timetable for activities, and helper roles. During circle time, they use language to remember the big ideas they are learning in this theme or that, and they hear language about new big ideas to come (e.g., the concept of force when you push, pull, and tug on objects, or the idea of buoyancy in exploring things that float or sink). Regular as day and night, circle time is a best practice that supports language use and conventions over and over again in a safe, secure environment where children feel a sense of belonging and importance.

Instructional Framework

Does circle time have an underlying instructional structure? Absolutely! It's one of the main reasons for its staying power in early childhood education. Each segment of circle time offers many opportunities for practicing speaking and listening skills—conversing, asking questions, providing information, and explaining and using language. When the time comes to talk about the day, for example, children regularly have the chance to use the language of everyday life as they tell the names of the day and month, describe the weather (sometimes in great detail), and comment on any special events of the day or the day before or coming up soon (with expressions of great anticipation).

Teaching Protocol

The regularity of circle time (nearly daily) makes this teaching practice seem effortless after a while. Yet teachers need to self-monitor the practice if they are to maximize its potential for daily oral language instruction. Consider the key teaching and learning features of the protocol as provided in Table 13 that ensure its high quality when used on a consistent basis.

A closer inspection of each segment provides some ideas about what you can look for when implementing circle time as a best practice. In the "Get Ready" segment, for example, you will want to make sure that you have a consistent routine during circle time so children know what to expect, and you will want to engage them in a motivating way. The "Talk About" and "Daily News" segments are prime times for children to talk a lot, so you will want to make sure you are encouraging and using lots of rich vocabulary and also facilitating the oral language skills of individual children. During the "Plan For" segment you should use theme-related materials to ready children for the upcoming day's activities, and highlight the daily schedule to support their own self-regulation. There is one word of caution: Do not spend too much time on any one segment. Set a brisk pace and transition smoothly from one to another. Young children, as you know, can only sit still (with attention and purpose) for a short while.

Table 13
Teaching Protocol for Circle Time

Segment	Teach	Learn
Get Ready	Focus attention to the day	Active listening
	Make personal connections	Share personal experiences
Talk About	Month, day, weather, current events	Words to describe time, temperature, environment
	Special events; related personal experiences	Words to describe activities; make connections
Daily News	Discussion *individual child shares; class discussion*	Rules of interaction Conversing about a topic Expressing; explaining ideas
Plan For	Daily schedule	Words for daily activities
	Theme-related ideas, facts, activities *read books, poems; do fingerplays; sing songs*	Content vocabulary

An Authentic Circle Time Lesson— "Meet Me and My Family"

Recall our brief discussion about authentic instruction earlier in this chapter. Our points revolved around the importance of engaging children in activities that result in accomplishments that are significant, worthwhile, and meaningful. Circle time—even though routine—includes opportunities for authentic language learning in a group setting. During circle time, children can develop the language of social interaction, share their personal experiences, and acquire vocabulary for daily life and school. Consider the lesson in Figure 12 as a fairly typical implementation of the circle time best practice for purposes of developing oral language. Pay particular attention to opportunities for children to explain events captured in family photographs and for peers to ask clarifying questions, such as "Where did you get that little dog?" and "How come you named him Moose?"

> During circle time, children can develop the language of social interaction, share their personal experiences, and acquire vocabulary for daily life and school.

Standards Connection

Developing social interaction skills is a top priority in any preschool program, and circle time is a best practice that helps you to accomplish this

Figure 12
Lesson Plan for Circle Time Using "Meet Me and My Family" Discussion

Circle Time: Meet Me and My Family

Objectives:
- Connect information and events to personal experience by sharing or commenting *[C2]
- Speak clearly and understandably to express ideas, feelings, and needs *[C3]
- Understand the meaning of words *[V1]
- Determine the meaning of new words with assistance or cues *[V5]

Day 1	GR: Recall favorite activities last week
	TA: Calendar and weather words; recent experiences
	DN: Ask children to tell where they live and number of family members
	PF: Read aloud *Lots of Moms*; highlight play area activities
Day 2	GR: Remember favorite parts of *Lots of Moms*
	TA: Calendar and weather words; map of family residences
	DN: Discuss note home to obtain a favorite family photo
	PF: Read aloud *Lots of Dads*; highlight key activities
Day 3	GR: Compare/contrast the two stories
	TA: Calendar and weather words; display of photos
	DN: Ask three or four children to explain their photo (who, what, when, where)
	PF: Read poem: "When Daddy was a little boy/All little boys were good/And did just what their parents said they should/And sometimes when I'm naughty/He takes me on his knee/And tells me, when he was little/How good he used to be" (author unknown)
Day 4–5	GR: Say special phrases/words from poem
	TA: Calendar and weather words; family names
	DN: Ask three or four children to explain their photo each day
	PF: Prepare the Big Photo Album of Families in the art area

Note. GR = get ready, TA = talk about, DN = daily news, PF = planning for (the day).

goal. Early educators know that children need many familiar situations where they can talk a lot to learn how to communicate effectively and appropriately in social contexts. When consistent, planned, and organized, circle time is an instructional practice that helps children to express their ideas, ask and answer questions, exchange experiences, and show consideration and respect for others. It exposes them to everyday words and new content words through discussion and conversation. Used regularly, circle time encompasses a wide range of oral language strategies and skills that preschoolers are expected to master at entry to kindergarten.

Dramatic Play

It is often said that young children learn best through play, and indeed this may be a great truth. Play is a satisfying activity where children can practice and extend what they know and can do. For this reason, play is referred to as a "leading" activity in early childhood, because play pulls forward children's physical, emotional, social, and cognitive development to higher levels of performance (Bodrova & Leong, 2007). Children really do benefit cognitively and socially from their active engagement in social play (Johnson et al., 2005). Thus, it is not wise to short-change dramatic play (or any other kind of play for that matter) in the preschool years.

Most of the time, children should be in charge of their own play— otherwise, it just isn't play. Yet at the same time, as an early educator, you should be guiding children toward more mature play by the end of the preschool years.

To be more specific, mature play is not simple play that consists of single actions and mimicry. Nor is it sequenced play where children assume a familiar role, follow a simple sequence of events, and use pretend props. Rather, it is play where children are able to do the following:

- Create an imaginary situation
- Use objects in a symbolic way
- Use language to enact play
- Take on explicit roles
- Follow implicit rules
- Persist at play (up to an hour or more)

To achieve mature play by the end of preschool many children need your support. You can help by providing props for play, by co-playing with children, and by leading play activity. Occasionally, children need your "lead" to recharge their play with novelty, challenge, and language.

Instructional Framework

Teachers should structure dramatic play so that children gain mature play skills that promote oral language development, yet maintain the free spirit of social play. Teachers can do this by providing enough structure to help children organize their thinking for play while allowing enough flexibility for their creativity (and language) to flourish. So how does this happen? Teachers must be intentional about connecting a dramatic play setting to the big ideas taught during shared book reading, circle time, and small-group instruction (e.g., play props and roles that are related to shared book reading sessions). In addition, teachers should actively support and guide social play toward specific instructional goals (e.g., learning new vocabulary words; Roskos and Christie, 2007). The BDA framework is a good fit for networking dramatic play with the broader preschool curriculum. It provides structure to support instructional goals yet gives children ample freedom to develop their own play scenarios (see the "Plan for Play" section in Chapter 4).

Before play, think about potential play topics linked to your current theme. Build children's background by taking real or virtual field trips (through technologies, such as Smart Boards), reading books, or hearing from invited guests. Have children help set up a dramatic play area related to the theme. They can make props, for example, or bring play resources from home.

During play, model mature play elements by introducing new words, new roles, and new routines that expand children's knowledge of the vocabulary and content understandings relevant to the theme. Encourage children to sustain their dramatic play over longer and longer periods of time.

After play, arrange to work with pairs or small groups. Help children remember their play and to connect it to the broader learning activities going on in the classroom. For example, children might talk about different roles played and say the special words they used in that role. They might find books and stories that remind them of their play, and pretend read or listen to them read aloud.

Networked dramatic play presents many opportunities for children to use vocabulary and oral language in integrative ways that increase their chances for learning through play and for retaining big ideas presented in other activities. Motivated to play well with others (so it is fun), they are pressed to use language for planning (e.g., "I'll feed the baby and then it will get sick, okay?"), deliberate remembering (e.g., "Always put the baby's bottle in the fridge, so we can find it."), problem solving (e.g., "Three kids is too many, so you can play over there.") and evaluating play activity (e.g., "Teacher…she's not doing what moms do."). Supporting dramatic play, therefore, is a best practice that creates a highly motivating context for oral language use.

Teaching Protocol

Considerable research documents the positive relationships between play and oral language development (Johnson et al., 2005). The Home School Study of Language and Literacy Development (Dickinson & Tabors, 2001), for example, examined the home and school literacy environments of low-income children from age 3 through kindergarten. The study reported consistent relationships between the language that children used during play and their performance on literacy and language measures. At age 3, children who engaged in more pretend talk during play were more likely to perform well on assessments of receptive vocabulary and narrative production (see Singer & Singer, 1990). Dickinson and Tabors (2001) also reported consistent links between play and long-term language growth. For example, the total number of words and the variety of words that children used during free play in preschool were positively related to their performance on language measures administered in kindergarten. Therefore, a more intentional approach to networking and supporting dramatic play can have real language learning consequences for the preschoolers in your classroom. The teaching protocol in Table 14 details what this might look like in the preschool setting (Neuman & Roskos, 2007).

When you use dramatic play as a part of your best practice repertoire, you are not "robbing" children of their time for play nor "stifling" their creativity. Rather you are using a highly effective practice that Bruner (1983) described as "leading from behind." When you support, coplay, and lead play, you are guiding children to more mature play, which paves the way for future creative expression as singer, writer, dancer, actor, builder, or scientist.

An Authentic Dramatic Play Lesson: Playing "Garage"

Over the years we have collected several wonderful play scenarios that we could share with you here, each and every one a true delight. In an age when play is too often set aside for preschool academics, we cherish the scenarios we have and continually seek new episodes. This one is a pretty good example of an authentic "play lesson" and emerged in a transportation theme during a time when a few parents were experiencing lots of car troubles (and expenses).

Table 14
Teaching Protocol for Dramatic Play

Phase	Teach	Learn
B	Name the theme—*ensure that it is a significant theme that develops content knowledge*	Focus attention on a topic
B	Tap children's background knowledge	Use language to remember details about a topic
B	Develop children's background knowledge	New words, phrases related to the topic
B	Select content vocabulary (e.g., *funnel, corks, salty water, density, oval, submarine*)	Associate content words with play props, roles, and routines
B	Make a "construction" plan for the play area	Focus attention on the play activity; use language for making and doing
D	Allow time for play (45–60 minutes)	Persist in play
D	Facilitate play as a supporter, co-player, and/or leader	Language for playing with others; for roles and activities
A	Follow through on play activity	Communicate experiences; use content vocabulary
A	Connect to other activities	Make connections to other learning experiences

Note. B = before reading, D = during reading, A = after reading.

What a terrific instructional practice—and so much fun for everyone. You have observed, no doubt, how dramatic play can become that nexus or crossroad where you can purposefully lead children toward new ideas, new words, new roles, and new language skills. At the same time you can respect what children already know and can do in creating their own play for the fun of it. On its serious side, dramatic play pushes children's language capabilities, builds their vocabulary, and advances their play to more mature forms. On its silly and fun side, it engages children in meaningful talk that makes them feel strong, powerful, proud and good. See Figure 13 for a lesson plan to use with children for the dramatic play scenario of "garage."

Figure 13
Lesson Plan for Dramatic Play Using "Garage" Scenario

Play Scenario: Playing Garage

Objectives:
- Understand the meaning of new words from context *[V1]
- Share findings of information through retelling, media, and play *[R-3]
- Speak clearly and understandably to express ideas, feelings, and needs *[C4]
- Initiate and sustain a conversation through turn-taking *[C-5]

Day 1	B: Name and discuss the theme so far—transportation
	D: Read *Sylvia's Garage* (Lee, 2002) informational book
	A: Discuss experiences with garages like Sylvia's
Day 2	B: Picture walk the book with the children's help; discuss new words *mechanic, engine, dipstick, oil*
	D: Invite children to help make a garage; ask about props; make a list and post it
	A: Provide supplies for props in art area; encourage prop-making (e.g., *pump, hose, car lift, signs*)
Day 3–4	B: Reread the book; discuss new words
	D: Discuss roles in a garage; make a list; use stick puppets to pretend and use language of the role
	A: More props; assemble the setting
Day 5	Play garage!

Note. B = before reading, D = during reading, A = after reading.

Standards Connection

You will not find much discussion about play in early learning standards and its role in language development (Christie & Roskos, 2006). This is unfortunate because both oral language and early literacy development turn on the expectation that children should know and be able to think with symbols—spoken and written. This requires the ability to separate thought from actions and objects in the immediate environment. For young children, this is a difficult distinction to make, because what is "here and now" has a strong pull on what they think and do. Collaborative socio-dramatic play, in particular, helps children to develop the ability to separate from the here and now ("Let's pretend we're at the beach, OK?"), to let one thing stand for another ("This block is a boat."), and to assume roles ("I'll be the mom; you be the dad."). For such play to occur, children must plan; they must regulate their talk and behaviors to keep the play going; they must communicate, using meaningful gestures and language. To play for the fun of it requires hard mental work—it puts symbolic thinking to the test and it exercises the creative mind. For these significant reasons, dramatic play is a best practice in developing oral language abilities and an essential one in meeting early learning standards.

FOR FURTHER EXPLORATION

Observe dramatic play in a preschool setting. Unobtrusively, record what you see and hear as the children interact with one another and the environment. Pay close attention to the guidelines for play presented in this chapter as you make observations. For example,

• Was the play mature or did it consist of simple actions and mimicry?

• Were there props in the environment to support use of language?

• Did the adult in the room coplay with the children?

• Was the play based on a theme that builds background knowledge?

• What content specific language was used in the play?

Following the observation, look at your field notes. What do you learn about the children's use of language in play? How did the adult support and encourage language use in play?

CHAPTER 6

Putting It All Together in the Early Childhood Classroom

In this book we have described different facets of joining oral language and early literacy in the early childhood classroom—from defining terms to using best practices. We took apart the joining framework first introduced in Chapter 1 and explored how language and literacy development processes work together, how to plan for instruction, how to create a supportive learning environment, and how to "tutor" language learning in interactions with young children. Yet we know that in real early childhood classrooms, oral language teaching and learning do not occur apart from other early learning domains. Rather, they are integrated into the full fabric of early education and care. Moreover, oral language is explored, experienced, learned, and used by the "whole child"—one who is healthy, safe, engaged, supported, and challenged (see www.wholechildeducation.org).

Now we need to describe what a framework that joins oral language and early literacy looks like in the classroom that supports the whole child. Putting it all together, we admit, is difficult to do in one short chapter. Thus, what follows is a slice of life taken from one day in one preschool teacher's classroom. What we hope to show is how this teacher brings the joining framework of language and literacy to life for the whole child.

The teacher is Shelley Adams, and her teaching assistant is Mari de Rivero. Mari completed her Child Development Associate credential and is currently enrolled in a two-year early childhood program at the local community college. This year, Shelley and Mari have a class of 20 preschoolers (13 girls, 7 boys), 6 of whom are African American, 3 of Middle Eastern descent, 10 of European American descent, and 1 of Asian descent.

Before the Everyday Routine Begins

Shelley recently attended a workshop on the early learning content standards, so she knows she has to spend time planning and making materials that will help children achieve standards-based performance indicators in language and literacy. Therefore, the everyday routine for children in Shelley's preschool classroom begins with lots of pre-planning and behind-the-scenes preparation.

Even before the preschool program officially started, she set up the physical environment as a place for her young children to play, learn, and have fun with friends. She organized the space and arranged the furniture in an inviting way. She used signage with complementary graphics to present information in easy-to-read ways that appeal to children (and are located within their line of sight). She took stock of her resources, including the size of her read-aloud collection (about 350 mixed-genre books), and reviewed the records of the children she will teach. She made "starter" nametags (to be completed by the children with their own "mark") and prepared essential charts for initial routines (e.g., the sign-in chart). With fellow teachers, she reviewed instructional priorities for the year (see Table 15) and coded the standards-based indicators as end-of-year outcomes (see Table 16). After this initial preparation, Shelley knows she will need to commit substantial time every day to planning for instruction across the program year.

The Start of One Day

One typical day begins as children hang up their coats or sweaters (with a little help from the adults) and then proceed to unpack and sort the contents of their book bags into one of two boxes located on a low table outside the preschool door. One box is labeled "Take-Home Books" with a photo of books. This is where children return the books they took home the night before. The other is labeled "Take-Home Folders" with a photo of folders. Here they return their home folder, which is one way Shelley stays in close communication with parents and caregivers.

Today, she is particularly pleased to see that Mina, who has recently arrived from Morocco, is able to put her books in the "Take-Home Books" box and her folder in the "Take-Home Folders" box. Having this routine to follow seems to have made Mina more comfortable in the classroom. Finally, the children put their names on the sign-in chart just inside the door, letting everyone know "I'm here today!" For Shelley and her teacher

Table 15
Teacher's List of Instructional Priorities for the School Year

Instructional Priority	Academic Quarter			
	1	2	3	4
Phonological Awareness				
Target 1: Sound/Word Discrimination	X			
Target 2: Rhyming		X	X	X
Target 3: Segmentation (word, syllable, onset-rime)			X	X
Target 4: Alliteration			X	X
Alphabet Knowledge				
Target 1: Letter Names (upper/lower)		8 U 5 L	15 U 12 L	20 U 17 L
Target 2: Letter Sounds			4	8
Print Awareness				
Target 1: Name	X			
Target 2: Print Functions		X	X	X
Target 3: Print Features/Conventions		X	X	X
Target 4: Sight Words			X	5–10
Target 5: Concept of Word				X
Target 6: Developmental Writing	X	X	X	X
Vocabulary				
Target 1: Labeling	X			
Target 2: Categorizing/Classifying		X		
Target 3: Expressive		X	X	X
Target 5: New Words (specialized)	X	X	X	X
Language Comprehension (Oral Language)				
Target 1: Listening to Stories and Books	X			
Target 2: Gaining/Reporting Information From Books		X	X	
Target 3: Retelling/Summarizing			X	X
Target 4: Making Connections	X	X	X	X
Target 5: Using Rules of Interaction	X	X	X	X

Note. Quarter 1 = Sept/Oct, Quarter 2 = Nov/Dec/Jan, Quarter 3 = Jan/Feb/Mar, Quarter 4 = Apr/May/June.

Table 16
Standards Coding Chart

Code	Standard
PA	*Phonemic Awareness, Word Recognition, and Fluency*
PA 1	Identify matching sounds and recognize rhymes in familiar stories, poems, songs, and words.
PA 2	Hear sounds in words by isolating the syllables of a word using snapping, clapping, or rhythmic movement (e.g., *cat, ap-ple*).
V	*Acquisition of Vocabulary*
V 1	Understand the meaning of new words from context of conversations, the use of pictures that accompany text, or the use of concrete objects.
RA	*Reading Applications: Informal, Technical, Persuasive, and Literary Text*
RA 1	Use pictures and illustrations to aid comprehension.
RA 2	Retell information from informational text.
WC	*Writing Conventions*
WC 1	Print letters of own name and other meaningful words with assistance using letterlike forms and/or conventional print.

Note. Provided by Shelley Adams, preschool teacher, Kenston Early Learning Center, Bainbridge, Ohio, USA.

assistant, Mari, the daily routine of signing in provides ongoing monitoring of children's name-writing skills: What alphabet letters they know and how well they can form them on paper. Mina's mother showed Shelley how to write Mina's name in Arabic. Shelley placed Mina's name in Arabic and in English over her cubby. Now Mina is working on writing her name using the English alphabet.

Shelley starts with children's names rather than a letter of the week because she knows that a child's own name is one of the best sources of alphabet knowledge for children, and that writing the initial letter of the child's name develops phoneme sensitivity (Bus & Both-de Vries, 2008). Moreover, if James knows that *J* is the first letter in his name, he might recognize it somewhere else in the preschool learning environment—on the felt board, in a book, on a chart, or in another child's name printed neatly on a cubby.

Shelley purposefully watches for children's letter-name and sound recognition in a variety of activities that center on their name writing. From these activities, all the children learn one another's names and the first letter that starts each other's names. At the same time, these activities give the children the opportunity to play with the sound that a letter makes, to feel the sound of each letter with their mouths and tongues, and to think of other words (real or made up) that also start with the same sound.

Inside the Room With Books and Puzzles

After signing in, the children move to tables and browse books or put puzzles together until all the others arrive. Easing into the day in this social way gives children a chance to greet each other ("Hi Sheona, my mommy bringed me today. Did you know?"), share happenings ("My Auntie JoJo is comin' for a real long time. She lives in Chicago, you know."), discuss what they see in the books they're reading ("Hey, Alex. Is this a dinosaur? Is this a pterodactyl?"), or work together to assemble a puzzle ("These is easy for us, right? Everythin's easy for us."). Shelley uses this time, too, to casually converse with the children one-on-one. When she stops at the table where Mina is working on a puzzle, she crouches down and says, "I see you have a puzzle, Mina. There are dogs and cats and mice and birds in your puzzle," pointing to each type of animal as she names them. Although Mina does not say anything to Shelley, she watches her teacher's face intently as she names the puzzle pieces. After Shelley leaves, Mina says some of the words softly to herself: "Dog, bird...."

And Now It's Circle Time

Clap, clap, sing, song, snap, snap, chant... Circle time opens with songs, rhymes, and finger-plays. Shelley introduces a new rhyme every week, but soon the children beg to open with their favorites every day—just for the sheer delight of saying or singing the words and sounds. Shelley, however, is quite deliberate about using this fun with songs, chants, and rhymes to build the phonological awareness of her preschoolers. She knows that their active engagement in singing, rhyming, and chanting helps them learn to listen for the sounds in language. Last week during circle time, Shelley noticed that Mina was joining in the rhymes for the first time. In fact, this was the first time that Shelley had heard Mina's voice in the classroom. Today, Mina wears a big smile as she shouts out the chants with the rest of the class.

After this warm-up activity, the schedule reader points to each event on the day's schedule while the rest of the group reads along. As they go, Shelley guides them to vary their volume as they chorally read, sometimes soft as snowflakes falling to the ground and sometimes loud like drums in a parade. The children are eager to explore the sounds of their own voices along with the printed words of the schedule.

The children settle and Shelley begins the shared reading session. The book today is the Big Book version of *Curious George* (Rey, 1941), a story about a mischievous monkey. Before reading, she engages the children's interest in the story and points out the particulars of title, author, and illustrator. She takes a picture walk through the story, pointing out the illustrations, highlighting key points and interesting new words. Then she reads, and as she goes she engages the children.

• • • • • • • • • • • • • • •

"What do you think will happen? How do you know that? This word is *curious*. You say it: *curious*. It means to be very interested in something. Turn and tell your friend what it means. Isn't that a funny word? Look at how it looks, so long with so many letters in it. Did I see an *s* in there by any chance? I'm a bit worried about George, aren't you? Well, now, wasn't that a great story? It reminds me of our field trip to the zoo a while back where we saw monkeys scampering and playing. What does it remind you of? Before we leave this story, today, let's do a picture walk again. This time, you help me out and we can retell this story."

• • • • • • • • • • • • • • •

On another day, Shelley will use a different after-reading activity, such as building vocabulary, reconstructing the story with sequence cards, reviewing the rhyming words in the book, or beginning a letter- or word-matching activity.

Shelley consciously varies the genres she reads to the children, and uses Big Book versions when available. Sometimes selections are stories and old favorites. The group adores *Lilly's Purple Plastic Purse* (Henkes, 1996) and *The Napping House* (Wood, 1984). At other times, she uses informational books that develop vocabulary and basic concepts, such as *Cats* (Gibbons, 1996), *Ducks Don't Get Wet* (Goldin, 1965), and *Spiders* (Resnick, 1996). To help children remember new words, she regularly discusses them with the children before, during, and after reading. She has them dramatize informational books to help them remember ideas, terms, and facts.

Circle time draws to a close with the question of the day: "Did you enjoy yesterday's program with Max the Moose?" The children respond with a resounding "Yes!" They then take turns bringing up a clothespin labeled with their name and attaching it to the "Yes" side of the chart. However, the results for yesterday's question, "Do you like chocolate milk?" were not unanimous, with 15 "Yes" votes and a surprising 6 "No" votes. As children post their votes, they slide their finger under Yes or No as they say it. Today, for the first time, Mina not only places her name on the chart but also says the word aloud: "Yes!" With Shelley's assistance, the children discuss today's results, which involves much talk and saying the word *unanimous*.

On to Play for More Learning

The children huddle around Shelley and Mari to share their play plans. They use the Play Area Chart to remind them where they played yesterday and to decide where they will start for the day. Several boys say they want to play in the block area, but Shelley reminds them that they have played there a lot, so maybe today they should try a new area. "How about the Discovery Area at the sand table where you can make wide roads and build tunnels with your bulldozers and dump trucks?" She turns to a few girls, encouraging them to think about the art area where they can make play props for the Health Foods Shop currently set up in the dramatic play area. Mari nods to Savannah. "Thank you, Savannah, for helping Mina choose the Health Foods Shop today." As the children finalize their decisions, they take their name tags to the play area of their choice.

James, Andrea, Mina, and Amerdeep head off for the dramatic play area, which is set up as a Health Foods Shop to further the current theme of "Healthy You, Healthy Me." Grocery packages, cookbooks, a "new healthy foods" demonstration area, recipes, notepads, coupons, and writing tools are available for play scenarios about cooking, food groups, and healthy eating. Shelley knows that the play talk that goes on here develops children's use of decontextualized language and provides opportunities for them to use new words, such as *fats*, *carbohydrates*, *proteins*, and *calories*. For the play to unfold, the children must listen to each other. As the children play, they are exposed to the culture, customs, and background knowledge of their friends. Although Mina does not add any talk to the play, she is a willing participant and listens carefully to the other children as they develop their play themes.

Jamal, Nicholas, and Blair head for the Block/Truck Construction area where there are all kinds of books on construction as well as paper and pencils to take work orders and a set of blueprints for reference. Another group moves toward the Writing Table stocked with all manner of writing supplies such as stencils, pens, pencils, envelopes, tactile letters, and different kinds of paper. Other materials are purposefully placed to provide practice with recognizing alphabet letters, making writing attempts, matching and sorting sounds, and other activities related to this week's objectives, which are as follows:

- Use new, topic-related words during play.
- Express ideas through drawing and writing.
- Play and manipulate sounds in words by saying, pronouncing, and sorting.
- Recognize alphabet letters in own name.

Sheona, Jaclyn, Isaiah, and Josie move to the Book Area because they like to play school. Today they will read and manipulate several interactive charts. "Little Miss Muffet" is especially popular because of that scary word, *spider*! After a few squeamish rounds with the word *spider*, the group splits, with some children inserting picture cards of other creatures into the Miss Muffet chart and others exploring different charts with familiar nursery rhymes, songs, and chants.

Shelley and Mari circulate among the play areas with several goals in mind. For brief periods, they may engage a few children in small-group instruction on a specific skill, such as hearing rhymes in words. Or each of them may involve one or more children in a read-aloud. At other times, they model language and play behaviors as needed. They support children's efforts and play along at their direction. While the children are deeply immersed in the flow of play, the teachers also informally assess the children's use of language and early literacy skills.

Bringing an end to play time, the teachers lead the children out the door to the playground for some time in the sunshine. They introduce a game—"Duck, Duck, Goose"—to the children. Shelley is pleased to see that Mina is an active participant in this game, as it had been difficult at first getting her involved in games. Today, she is as eager as the other children to take her turn, touching each child and saying "Duck," until she comes to the one she wants to pick as the "Goose." After a few rounds, Shelley asks Jared to follow her lead, which he does with a voice of great authority.

A Break for Snack

The children assemble for snack time. Today, like every day, Shelley and Mari set out the snack with a sign that tells "How Many" snack items each child should count out and enjoy. The numeral is clearly written followed by dots that children can count. The teachers are deliberately building children's math skills by handling snack time in this way. Counting to 10, touching objects and saying the number names, identifying and naming numerals, and demonstrating a one-to-one correspondence when counting are important early learning math content standards addressed during this simple snack-counting routine.

Conversations flow as the teachers pose questions about the snack ("These baby carrots are crunchy, don't you think?"), prompt the sharing of preferences or similar foods served at home ("Elijah, you were telling me once that your grandma makes the best carrot cake. Is that right?"), and talk about what play centers the children played in today ("I was wondering, Rosa and Spencer, if you fixed a lot of cars today.").

One More Read-Aloud Before the Close of the Day

After their healthy snack of carrots, raisins, wheat crackers, and apple juice, the children gather for another read-aloud. One small group joins Shelley, and another goes with Mari. Today is the second read of *Raccoon on His Own* (Arnosky, 2001) with Shelley and of *Knuffle Bunny* (Willems, 2004) with Mari. This time, the children will add details to the story problem, tell portions aloud, and ask why questions, such as "Why is Daddy mad at Trixie?" (in *Knuffle Bunny*) or "Why is he [raccoon] scared?" (in *Raccoon on His Own*). After a third read on another day, the pair will rotate groups, so all the children have the chance to participate interactively in both stories. Shelley is considering using a story drama technique with her group as a way to re-enact the story (Charters & Gately, 1986). She likes this technique because it helps the children become acquainted with the plot structure of the story: setting, the problem, the buildup of tension, the turning point, and finally the resolution.

The Close of the Day

It is nearly time to depart, so the children all gather as Shelley passes around the Mystery Box for the children to explore. They put their hands in the box: "So, what do you think it is? What does it feel like? Tell me some more. Savannah said it felt like it had ridges. What do you think she meant?" The children feel with their hands and talk. "It feels like a round thing. Does it go on our trucks? It has hard spots." They listen intently for more clues. All the while, Shelley knows that she is helping the children learn to listen, to use descriptive words, and to express their thinking with language.

She continues to encourage talk for a short bit and then turns to the easel for some writing. "Let's record this mystery," she says, and she begins to write what the children have to say. Alex says, "It feels like a round thing." Shelley talks about the words as she writes, "It is a short word and I hear a /t/ at the end. I need to leave a space before I start to write *feels*." She finishes the sentence and then takes another suggestion from the children. After three or four sentences, the children have enough clues to identify the mystery object—a small tire that fell off one of the tractors in the block area. "We were looking for that tire for a long time," Isaiah says. Missing object found and mystery solved! At the completion of this whole-group time, children choose take-home books, get their mail, and then go to their cubbies and pack their backpacks for dismissal.

Today and Thereafter

After the children have gone, Shelley and Mari tidy up the room and then turn to an accounting of the day. Today, like every day, they use their progress-monitoring tools to keep track of how children are doing in terms of instructional goals. Shelley writes up her anecdotal notes, while Mari collects work samples, like language experience stories that children have dictated during the day. Later these items are posted to each child's "working" portfolio. In addition, they conduct a Five-Minute Friday Conference every week with three or four children who need more support. Based on the weekly objectives, they check these children's letter name knowledge, knowledge of vocabulary words, and rhyming and alliteration skills. In these routine ways, the pair keeps track of the children's language development and early literacy learning and monitor the effectiveness of their own instruction.

Teachers Continue to Learn, Too

Although it may look simple, what Shelley and Mari do each day is not. Teachers like Shelley depend on many kinds of knowledge to meet their responsibilities of helping young children gain oral language and early literacy as first steps in school readiness. Today's teachers and teacher assistants not only must be able to create stimulating and orderly early learning environments, but they also must help diverse groups of children learn more complex content and develop a wider range of oral language and early literacy skills. For this, initial preparation is not enough nor can experience alone supply adequate knowledge and skills. To be successful teachers and teacher assistants, early educators need to engage in ongoing professional learning to add to their knowledge and skills across their careers.

Learning About Young Children

Teachers and teacher assistants are busy people, and the time they spend in professional development must be time well spent. Priority should be given to learning more about young learners and how they develop. School readiness in the early years involves the whole child. To be effective, early childhood professionals need to be able to support children's development across different growth areas that interact with one another, including physical, socio-emotional, and cognitive domains. The growing diversity of families and children also requires understanding cultural differences that may make a difference in children's development.

To help all children learn language and literacy, early childhood educators need to be prepared to recognize the unique ways each child has learned to learn and to support each child's learning needs for language and literacy growth. Teachers and their assistants need to know about language development, including second-language acquisition—and to be especially concerned with promoting children's communication skills and building their store of vocabulary.

Learning More About Curriculum

Teachers and teacher assistants need to know about early learning content standards at national, state, and local levels because these provide the general guidelines about what to teach and why. Time must be given to learning how to read and interpret standards frameworks, how to use them in planning, and how to approach them with particular groups of children.

More than ever before, teachers are faced with making curriculum decisions about oral language and early literacy materials for their classrooms. How well do these new material resources meet the standards? Are they research-based? Are they appropriate for these children in this community? How well do they fit into our program? How do they support youngsters at risk? Questions like these require teachers to develop a curricular vision that keeps standards-based goals *and* developmentally appropriate instruction in sight when making decisions about materials and instructional approaches. In the end, the best preschool program is one constructed by teachers in response to adopted standards, particular needs and prior experiences of the children, and the resources and demands of the local community. Strong preschool language and literacy programs are assembled and built, not bought wholesale and applied.

Learning More About Skillful Teaching

To provide effective oral language instruction that supports early literacy, teachers and their assistants need to cultivate an ever-deepening understanding of how young children make sense of (and also confuse) language and literacy concepts. Knowing that most 4-year-olds hold a very fragile sense of word, for example, underlies effective instruction in the alphabetic principle at this age.

Further, teachers in collaboration with their assistants must apply effective practices to meet a wide range of diverse learning needs among young children, which involves constructing a culturally responsive curriculum, as well as an inclusive one. To help young learners with all their many differences acquire common, high-level oral language and early literacy concepts and skills, teachers need to be skilled assessors who can use many different assessment tools. They must command a repertoire of formative assessment strategies, including ways to help young children acquire self-regulation skills. For all this to happen day-in and day-out, teachers must be fluent in sound classroom management techniques and well-organized to ensure a productive learning environment.

Venues for Professional Learning

Fortunately, opportunities for professional learning in early literacy abound these days and are increasingly accessible to early childhood educators everywhere. You may be fortunate enough to become involved in a federal program, like Early Reading First, or a large-scale study sponsored through the National Institute of Child Health and Human Development (NICHD). You may choose to enroll in a professional education program to gain a new credential or degree. (Many find this an attractive route because it can lead to new job opportunities.)

Then there is an ever-growing menu of learning options online. You can take an online course, such as those offered through PBS Teacher Line (www.pbs.org).

Professional organizations, such as the National Association for the Education of Young Children (NAEYC) and the International Reading Association (IRA), also provide conference opportunities for learning where you can attend workshop sessions, discuss hot topics with colleagues, and purchase top-notch professional books for your own personal learning.

Of course, your own workplace is also a place where you can participate in periodic training workshops and study groups. Why not start a book club and chose a professional book to read and discuss every month?

No matter the venue, the important point is that you continue to learn about young children's language and literacy development and apply this knowledge to your own continuous improvement as an early literacy teacher. An effective professional development program should have the following characteristics (adapted from Hawley & Valli, 1999):

- Connects content and activities to standards of early learning
- Provides opportunities to practice new skills
- Models specific instructional techniques to use
- Builds a community of early educators
- Includes a follow-up to support classroom practice

We have one last piece of advice before you close this book: When making decisions about how to spend your time learning, keep these characteristics of quality professional development in mind. You are worth it.

Conclusion

We appreciate the opportunity to visit Shelley, Mari, and their 20 pre-schoolers, if only for a short time. We learned from their example that preschool teachers and teacher assistants, working together, can join oral language and early literacy in their settings to help children learn language, learn about language, and learn through language. Guided by early learning expectations in language and literacy, they are planful. Deliberate in their choices of activities, they are purposeful. Genuinely active in their teaching role, they are playful. As a result, all young children grow more capable in their abilities to talk, read, and write—and to flourish in school.

My ABCs

A Is for Assessments

This section provides a quick reference to language and early literacy assessments available for use in preschool programs. Educators can use the listing as a starting point in the decision-making process related to selecting assessment measures for purposes of screening, monitoring, and evaluating program outcomes.

Assessment of Literacy and Language
website: pearsonassess.com/HAIWEB/Cultures/en-us/Productdetail .htm?Pid=015–8074–742andMode=summary
The Assessment of Literacy and Language (ALL) aids in early detection of language disorders in preschoolers through first-graders that could lead to reading difficulties. ALL assesses spoken language and written language skills, including listening comprehension, language comprehension, semantics, syntax, phonological awareness, alphabetic principles/phonics, and concepts about print. With ALL, you can identify language disorders, language and emergent literacy deficits, emergent literacy deficits, and weak language and emergent literacy.

Early Literacy Advisor (ELA)
Mid-continent Research for Education and Learning (McREL)
4601 DTL Boulevard
Suite 500
Denver, CO 80237, USA
phone: 303-337-0990
website: www.mcrel.org/programs/literacy/ela/index.asp
ELA is a research-based assessment system that assists classroom teachers in assessing and promoting early literacy development in children ages 4–6. ELA creates an informative student profile that combines an in-depth analysis of a child's current level of literacy development with individualized, research-based teaching suggestions. Profiles are delivered to teachers

within days, making them useful for immediate, powerful intervention and as a tool to gauge student's progress toward state and local standards. The core of the ELA is its JAVA-based "expert system," which makes connections between raw assessment data and developmentally appropriate teaching techniques, assisting teachers in selecting strategies most likely to advance the literacy development of each student, tracking each student's results and building a personal database.

Early Literacy Skills Assessment (ELSA)
website: www.highscope.org/Content.asp?ContentId=114
ELSA is an authentic assessment in the form of a children's storybook designed to measure the emerging literacy skills of children attending early childhood programs. ELSA assesses comprehension, phonological awareness, the alphabetic principle, and concepts about print. To conduct the assessment, a teacher reads the story with an individual child, stopping when prompted to ask questions or elicit ideas. To evaluate the child's progress, the assessment is repeated at the end of the year with the same storybook.

ELLCO Pre-K
website: www.brookespublishing.com/store/books/smith-ellco/index.htm
Early Language and Literacy Classroom Observation (ELLCO) is a research-based tool used to identify classroom practices and environmental supports that promote early language and literacy development. The ELLCO looks at elements of the classroom environment and elements of language, literacy, and curriculum to measure five key literacy elements: classroom structure, curriculum, the language environment, books and book reading opportunities, and print and early writing supports. With ELLCO Pre-K, preschools and elementary schools will have the information they need to determine the effectiveness of their classroom environments, strengthen the quality of their programs and teaching practices, and improve young children's early literacy outcomes.

Get It Got It Go!
website: ggg.umn.edu
Get It Got It Go! (GGG) is a comprehensive tool that is useful in measuring children's risk and progress in critical language and early literacy indicators from birth to age 8. These individual growth and development indicators are picture naming, rhyming, and alliteration. GGG allows families and

educators to enter individual child data, get score recording forms, generate graphical reports to monitor the developmental growth of individual children and groups of children, and determine if intervention is necessary. The system also includes solutions-oriented assessments allowing families and early childhood and early elementary educators to identify features of classroom and home settings they can change to improve children's developmental outcomes. Additionally, GGG features dynamic data management tools to use online.

Get Ready to Read! Screening Tool
National Center for Learning Disabilities (NCLD)
381 Park Avenue South,
Suite 1401
New York, NY 10016, USA
phone: 888-575-7373
website: www.getreadytoread.org
Get Ready to Read! is a nationwide campaign to provide parents and early childhood care providers with understanding of the skills and knowledge 4-year-olds need to be ready to learn to read in kindergarten. One part of this initiative is the development of this research-based screening tool, a 20-item instrument that focuses on the "inside-out" skills in three areas: print knowledge, emergent writing, and linguistic awareness. By pointing to a series of icons, children can demonstrate skills in these areas. The tool is a reliable, research-based series of questions for children in the year before they enter kindergarten to determine whether they have the early literacy skills they need to become readers.

PALS
website: pals.virginia.edu
The Phonological Awareness Literacy Screening (PALS) provides a comprehensive assessment of young children's knowledge of the important literacy fundamentals that are predictive of future reading success. PALS consists of three instruments: PALS-PreK (for preschool students), PALS-K (for kindergartners), and PALS 1–3 (for students in grades 1–3). PALS assessments are designed to identify students in need of additional reading instruction beyond that provided to typically developing readers and informs teachers' instruction by providing them with explicit information about their students' knowledge of literacy fundamentals. Mid-year assessment and PALS Quick Checks allow for ongoing student progress monitoring throughout the year.

Peabody Picture Vocabulary Test—Third Edition

website: ags.pearsonassessments.com/group.asp?nGroupInfoID=a12010

PPVT-III is the leading wide-range measure of receptive vocabulary for standard English and a screening test of verbal ability. This individually administered, norm-referenced instrument is offered in two parallel forms—IIIA and IIIB—for reliable testing and retesting. PPVT-III features objective and rapid scoring, numerous stimulus words, an administration time of 10–15 minutes, items reviewed by a multicultural panel, and illustrations for better gender and ethnic balance.

Preschool PQA

website: www.highscope.org/Content.asp?ContentId=2

The PQA is a rating instrument designed to evaluate the quality of early childhood programs and identify staff training needs that covers 63 dimensions of program quality in seven domains: learning environment, daily routine, adult–child interaction, curriculum planning and assessment, parent involvement and family services, staff qualifications and development, and program management. Raters observe the program and interview the appropriate staff members. They record supporting evidence for each row (component) of every item and read the indicators (definitions and examples) for that row and check the one box per row that best reflects the supporting evidence. Then, using the scoring rules, they circle one item rating for the item as a whole.

Teacher Rating of Oral Language and Literacy (TROLL)

Center for the Improvement of Early Reading Achievement (CIERA)
University of Michigan, School of Education, Room 2002 SEB
610 East University Avenue
Ann Arbor, MI 48109-1259, USA
phone: 734-647-6940
website: www.ciera.org
www.ciera.org/library/reports/inquiry-3/3-016/3-016.pdf

The Teacher Rating of Oral Language and Literacy (TROLL) is a rating tool designed to provide preschool teachers with a way to track the language and literacy development of individual children in their classrooms. TROLL contains three subscales: language use, reading, and writing. Introductory questions determine the language(s) the child speaks and his or her comprehension and production abilities in English. Teachers are given the opportunity to rate English and native language competence. The tool has 25 items, and teachers can do the rating in 5–10 minutes without prior training.

Woodcock-Johnson III NU Tests of Achievement
website: www.riverpub.com/products/wjIIIAchievement/index.html
The WJIII NU Tests of Achievement can be administered in about five minutes and has two parallel forms (A and B) that are divided into two batteries—Standard and Extended. The 10 tests in the WJIII NU Tests of Achievement include 7 new tests; 8 new clusters; 4 oral language tests; expanded broad achievement clusters with 3 tests to measure basic skills, fluency, and application; a revised procedure for evaluating intra-achievement discrepancies that now include oral language; and expanded reading tests containing more items to measure early reading performance. Professionals can use the WJIII NU to diagnose learning disabilities, determine learning variations, plan educational programs, plan individual programs, assess growth, provide psychometric training, provide guidance in educational and clinical settings, and conduct research.

B Is for (Professional) Books

Teachers of young children need to remain current on key topics in early literacy teaching and learning. This section lists professional books for a well-stocked professional library and for use in book study groups.

Armbruster, B.B., Lehr, E., & Osborn, J. (2003). *A child becomes a reader: Birth through preschool.* **Washington, DC: National Institute for Literacy.**
website: www.nifl.gov/partnershipforreading/publications/html/parent_guides/birth_to_pre.html
A good resource for parents that includes a short summary of what scientific research says about how children learn to read and write, things you can do with your children from birth through age 2 to help them become readers, things you can do with your children between the ages of 3–4 and what to look for in quality day care centers and preschools to help your children become readers, a list of helpful terms, and ideas for books to read and organizations to contact if you would like more help or information.

Bennett-Armistead, V.S., Duke, N.K., & Moses, A.M. (2005). *Literacy and the youngest learner: Best practices for educators of children from birth to 5.* **New York: Scholastic.**
Literacy and the Youngest Learner: Best Practices for Educators of Children From Birth to 5 begins with an argument for offering children print-rich

activities and environments based on goals set forth by the International Reading Association, the National Association for the Education of Young Children, and the National Research Council. From there, the book focuses on enjoyable and effective ways to build essential skills such as oral language and phonological awareness, and ways to create dramatic play areas, book nooks, writing centers, and other educational spaces.

Dickinson, D.K., & Tabors, P.O. (2001). *Beginning literacy with language: Young children learning at home and school*. Baltimore: Paul H. Brookes.

Based on research gathered in the Home-School Study of Language and Literacy Development, this volume reveals for readers the relationship the authors found between critical, early interactions and children's kindergarten and literacy skills. The volume explores both the home and the school environments of children ages 3–5, especially how families talk to their young children during everyday activities and how teachers strive to support students' development at school.

Fox, M. (2001). *Reading magic: Why reading aloud to our children will change their lives forever*. Orlando, FL: Harcourt.

In this book, Fox speaks of when, where, and why to read aloud and demonstrates how to get the most out of a read-aloud session. The author discusses secrets of reading, offers guidance on defining and choosing good books, and addresses the challenges that can arise while reading aloud. Filled with practical advice, activities, and inspiring read-aloud miracles, this book is a favorite of educators, parents, and anyone interested in how children learn to read. The book reaffirms the educational benefits of reading aloud while reminding us that it can also bring intense happiness to both children and adults.

McGee, L.M., & Richgels, D.J. (2003). *Designing early literacy programs: Strategies for at-risk preschool and kindergarten children*. New York: Guilford.

Taking professionals and students step-by-step through conceptualizing, planning, and implementing an effective early literacy program, this book focuses on preventing reading difficulties and promoting success in at-risk 3- to 5-year-olds. Ideas for tailoring instruction to the needs of culturally and linguistically diverse learners are accompanied by clear assignment guidelines. A comprehensive framework is delineated for helping young children construct meaning from different kinds of texts, develop key oral language skills, and learn concepts about print and the alphabet. The book also offers practical suggestions for setting up literacy activities and arranging the classroom environment and offers depictions of a preschool and kindergarten classroom in action.

McGee, L.M., & Richgels, D.J. (2008). *Literacy's beginnings: Supporting young readers and writers* **(5th ed.). Needham, MA: Allyn & Bacon.**
This book clearly and simply explains issues addressed in Reading First and Early Reading First legislation that affect the reading instruction of young children. Aligned with the findings of the National Reading Panel, it focuses on child-centered instruction in phonemic awareness, phonics, decoding, comprehension, and interpretation.

Pianta, R.C., Cox, M.J., & Snow, K.L. (Eds.). (2007). *School readiness and the transition to kindergarten in the era of accountability.* **Baltimore: Paul H. Brookes.**
In this book, more than 30 highly respected experts give readers the latest information on topics surrounding early childhood education and kindergarten transition. It covers how to make the most of learning opportunities in early childhood classrooms, build stronger connections between early childhood and elementary education programs, and work to close racial and ethnic gaps in school readiness. It also addresses health, neurological development, and other factors that affect school readiness and academic success.

Schickendanz, J.A. (1999). *Much more than the ABCs: The early stages of reading and writing.* **Washington, DC: National Association for the Education of Young Children.**
Based on the premise that children need a solid foundation of literacy knowledge and skill to succeed, this book provides a comprehensive introduction to literacy development from infancy through preschool with an emphasis on age-appropriate methods, books, and materials for encouraging emergent literacy for parents and teachers. The author offers concrete suggestions, grounded in research and expert practice, to ensure that children from infancy through the early years not only learn to read and write, but also enjoy doing it. Bibliographies for age-appropriate children's books are listed throughout the book.

Vukelich, C., Christie, J.F., & Enz, B. (2008). *Helping young children learn language and literacy: Birth through kindergarten.* Boston: Pearson.

This book blends a constructivist/emergent literacy perspective with scientifically based instructional practices that have proven successful in supporting young children's reading, writing, and speaking development. The authors describe a continuum of approaches to reading instruction, ranging from emergent literacy to scientifically based reading research. They advocate a combination of meaningful engagements with print and age-appropriate instruction on core literacy skills. There is also extensive coverage of working with children from diverse backgrounds, family literacy, and assessment strategies that can be used to inform instruction.

C Is for Curriculum Resources

This section provides a sampler of curriculum resources that help to create a supportive learning environment for language and literacy in preschool settings. Effective programs use high quality materials that support and enrich instruction. Educators can use this list as a reference tool when considering curriculum resources for their programs.

Alphabet Soup
website: www.alphabet-soup.net/
Alphabet Soup is designed to help children 0–8 years old improve their literacy skills in a fun and entertaining way. Alphabet Soup features the Kindergarten Kafe, thematic units, teacher and parent resources, literature, recipes, fun and humor, crafts, and special pages for mainly 3–5-year-olds. It has been created so that children can learn in a safe online environment.

Between the Lions
website: pbskids.org/lions/index.html
Between the Lions is funded in part by a Ready To Learn cooperative agreement with the U.S. Department of Education through PBS and aims to foster literacy skills in 4–7-year-olds. The goals of the series are to dramatize the benefits of reading; show that learning to read and spell can be a struggle, but a worthwhile one; show that there are many reasons to write; introduce new vocabulary words and their meanings; and show how words work through phonemics, alphabetic principle, and spelling conventions. Between the Lions also gives young viewers a chance to have meaningful

and manageable reading experiences by using keywords in simple, decodable, connected text onscreen. The website reinforces the literacy mission of the PBS series and is designed to be used by an adult and child together. The website includes read-along stories, interactive games, printables, clips, songs, and resources for both parents and teachers.

Building Language for Literacy
website: teacher.scholastic.com/products/activitites/bll/index.htm
Building Language for Literacy is a research-based program that develops children's oral language and early literacy skills and can serve as the basis for your early literacy curriculum or can be integrated with a current one. With Building Language for Literacy, you can prepare children for reading success using high-quality literature, songs and poems, rich vocabulary, and language-loving characters. At the same time, you can foster children's awareness in other domains as the program is integrated with science, social studies, math, writing, music, and other curriculum and content areas.

Cecil, N.L. (2007). *Striking a balance: Best practices for early literacy (3rd ed.). Scottsdale, AZ: Holcomb Hathaway.*
Designed primarily as a textbook for the preservice teacher on reading instruction in the primary grades, this book focuses on whether phonics or the whole-language approach is the best method for teaching children to read. The author brings some order to this chaos of opinions by focusing on practices that either have been tested through research or identified by practitioners who have a track record of helping children with reading difficulties. A "List of Activities" organized by chapter follows the Table of Contents and will aid the practicing teacher in the use of this book as a reference tool. Helpful appendices also provide such items as lists of children's books for various teaching strategies, recommended books for teachers, websites for use with students or as aids to the teacher, and lists of commercial and informal assessment instruments.

The Creative Curriculum® for Preschool
website: www.teachingstrategies.com/page/CCPS_Content.cfm
The Creative Curriculum® for Preschool translates new research and theory from the field of early childhood education into a practical, easy-to-understand approach to working with children and their families. It is a comprehensive curriculum with a clear organizational structure and a particular focus on interest areas. The structure of The Creative Curriculum®

for Preschool includes the following sections: theory and research, how children develop and learn, the learning environment, what children learn, the teacher's role, the family's role, and interest areas.

DLM Early Childhood Express Curriculum

website: www.wrightgroup.com/family.html?PHPSESSID=ae71226df93c0 a0211ac7a57f5dDLMEarlyChildhoodExpress.pdf

The DLM Early Childhood Express, published by the Wright Group of McGraw-Hill, is a comprehensive, research-based program that has nine thematic units with lesson plans. DLM Learning Express links language and early literacy, math, science, social studies, fine arts, health and safety, personal and physical development, and technology. Materials include lesson plans with 36 weekly themes that include activities to help children make connections, expand on their experiences, and build new knowledge on a variety of topics.

ELSB—Early Literacy Skills Builder

website: www.attainmentcompany.com/xcart/product.php ?productid=16526

ELSB is a language-rich literacy curriculum for children ages 5 to 10 with moderate to severe developmental disabilities, including autism. The Early Learning Skills Builder program incorporates systematic instruction to teach both print and phonemic awareness. ELSB is a multi-year program with seven distinct levels and ongoing assessments so students progress at their own pace.

Growing Readers Early Literacy Curriculum

website: secure.highscope.org/ProductCart/pc/viewPrd.asp ?idproduct=527

The Growing Readers Early Literacy Curriculum is an early literacy curriculum in the form of 90 small-group activities, as well as other support materials, which addresses the four key areas of early literacy learning—comprehension, phonological awareness, alphabetic principle, and concepts about print. The Growing Readers Early Literacy Curriculum features a comprehensive teacher guide, including complete instructions, background information, scope and sequence, individual and group progress profiles and activity log; over 90 small-group activity cards with detailed instructions for classroom activities; short activity and teaching strategy cards; letter links cards; quick look cards; support cards; and a richly varied collection of nine new and classic children's books.

Growing Readers Early Literacy Curriculum: Research-Based Small-Group Instructional Activities for Preschoolers
website: www.highscope.org/Content.asp?ContentId=321
The first set of activities in the Growing Readers Early Literacy Curriculum (GRC) is now available in kit form with an accompanying set of children's books. This is a developmentally sensitive curriculum that grows from reading research and the principles of active learning. The GRC takes place during small-group time in preschool and kindergarten classrooms. Activities are presented on three developmental levels. The activities are designed to systematically support the growth of young children's early literacy skills in the areas of comprehension, alphabetic principle, phonological awareness, and concepts about print.

Interactive Technology Literacy Curriculum
website: www.wiu.edu/users/itlc/itlc_workshops.html
The Interactive Technology Literacy Curriculum online is a service for families and early childhood professionals and is sponsored by the Center for Best Practices in Early Childhood Education at Western Illinois University. ITLC provides online workshops that focus on the use of technology as a tool to assist young children with disabilities in achieving developmental goals. This site, which is free to use, is funded as part of a research project through the U.S. Department of Education, but registration and login are required for access. The available workshops are Literacy Foundations, Literacy Environments, Children's Software, Technology Integration, Authoring Software, and Literacy Assessment.

Knapp-Philo, J. (2008). *Celebrating language and literacy for infants, toddlers and twos* (computer software). Rohnert Park: California Institute on Human Services, Sonoma State University.
These videos show how early literacy skills develop within the context of caring relationships and experiences with families, providers, and communities. The first building blocks of language and literacy are shown to be supported by adults who intentionally facilitate children's interests within environments rich in opportunities. The videos also provide examples of the many ways that language and literacy develop in a variety of cultures and languages and demonstrate how adults can help very young children read the world around them. Furthermore, the videos exemplify how everyday routines, experiences, and environments provide the tools for literacy through nurturing relationships; talking and listening; writing; and experiencing symbols, sounds, and rhyme.

Literacy Center Education Network
website: www.literacycenter.net
The Early Childhood Education Network has the goal that all children will be able to access the same high-quality, research-based, education material and offers nine basic activities in four languages (English, Spanish, German, and French). Through simply designed activities, children learn to recognize colors, phonemes, letters, numbers, and shapes and to use computer keyboard basics. The Parents and Teachers section explains how each lesson is part of the early language experience.

Lybolt, J., Armstrong, J., Techmanski, K.E., & Gottfred, C. (2007). *Building language throughout the year: The preschool early literacy curriculum.* **Baltimore: Paul H. Brookes.**
This book is a valuable resource for the facilitation of language and literacy skill development for any preschool classroom. The focus on vocabulary in each of the lessons helps to address a key feature of literacy development that is often overlooked in other curricula. This emphasis is supported by a review of research included in the text with specific suggestions for teachers to follow to maximize the vocabulary development and subsequent learning taking place in their classrooms. The authors also provide definitions and descriptions of the teachers' roles in using the *Building Language Through the Years* curriculum, focusing on the need for assessment, preparation of the physical aspects of the learning environment, appropriate lesson planning, implementation of the lessons, and the importance of both explicit and opportunistic instruction to scaffold literacy learning.

McGregor, T. (2007). *Comprehension connections: Bridges to strategic reading.* **Portsmouth, NH: Heinemann.**
This book is a resource for educators developing effective curriculum plans to enhance reading comprehension for elementary readers. The author shares some of her curriculum plans, lessons, activities, and projects to provide concrete examples for children as they develop skills as readers and thinkers, and she introduces her four-stage "launching sequence" consisting of *concrete experiences*, *sensory exercises*, *wordless picture books*, and *time for text* within a frame of seven fundamental concepts for developing strategic reading skills: metacognition, schema, inferring, questioning, determining importance, visualizing, and synthesizing. These project-based lesson plans are designed to help students transition

from an abstract and distant concept into a more tangible reading experience that incorporates strategic thinking about reading while instilling a sense of independence for the developing reader.

National Institute for Early Education Research
website: nieer.org
The National Institute for Early Education Research supports early childhood education initiatives by providing objective, nonpartisan information based on research. The goal of NIEER is to produce and communicate the knowledge base required to ensure that every American child can receive a good education at ages 3 and 4. The Institute seeks to provide policymakers with timely information addressing the practical problems they face. The Institute offers independent research-based advice and technical assistance to four primary groups: policymakers, journalists, researchers, and educators.

Notari-Syverson, A., O'Connor, R., & Vadasy, P. (2007). *Ladders to literacy: A preschool activity book.* **Baltimore: Paul H. Brookes.**
This book contains nearly 300 pages of instructional games, story-related activities, classroom lessons, and play ideas to engage kindergarteners and even older or special needs students in preliteracy skill development. This structured, scaffolded program targets print awareness, phonological awareness, and oral language skills, while fostering in young children a love of literacy and learning. The Appendix provides a useful guide for involving parents in literacy development in the home and community, and also includes a list of children's books to reinforce such concepts as alphabet, alliteration, syllable segmentation, rhyming, and oral expression.

Open Court Reading Pre-K
website: www.opencourtresources.com/ocr/prek/index.html
Open Court Reading Pre-K is a research-based curriculum designed for use with preschoolers. It includes eight units organized around typical preschool topics: I'm Special, Families Everywhere, All Kinds of Friends, Helping Hands, Let's Go, Senses, At the Farm, and Changes. Each unit consists of 20 daily lessons with two large-group activities and one small-group activity. Writing activities are also included and integrated into the lessons. Open Court Reading Pre-K was designed to teach children to decode and comprehend in an efficient manner so that they can read a variety of quality literature.

Opening the World of Learning (OWL)

website: www.pearsonlearning.com/microsites/owl/main.cfm

Opening the World of Learning (OWL) is a comprehensive early literacy-focused program designed for use with preschoolers. OWL has six units, each with four weeks of activities: Family, Friends, Wind and Water, The World of Color, Shadows and Reflections, and Things That Grow. The research-based activities promote learning in all content areas and build personal and social skills. Opening the World of Learning has fun activities and experiences for learning academic and social skills that lead to school success.

PBS Parents: Reading and Language

website: www.pbs.org/parents/readinglanguage

Inspiration for Reading and Language comes from PBS's belief that learning to read is one of the most meaningful and powerful experiences that a parent and child can share. Designed for parents of children from birth through 8 years of age, this site informs parents about how literacy development occurs at various ages, provides parents with some guidelines for how they can support children's literacy development at each stage, and offers some carefully reviewed resources parents may find helpful as they raise eager readers and writers. When you visit Reading and Language, you can select an age to find information specifically relevant to your child's developmental stage. In addition, the site features articles presenting practical information and new research findings.

Reading Is Fundamental

website: www.rif.org

Reading Is Fundamental, Inc. (RIF), founded in 1966, motivates children to read by working with them, their parents, and community members to make reading a fun and beneficial part of everyday life. RIF's highest priority is reaching underserved children from birth to age 8. Through community volunteers in every state and U.S. territory, RIF provides 4.6 million children with 16 million new, free books and literacy resources each year. Reading Is Fundamental, Inc. is the nation's largest nonprofit children's literacy organization. Filled with RIF favorites, including reading activity calendars, read-aloud stories, Spanish-language resources, literacy games, newsletters, and summer reading resources, this is a great early language site.

Rief, S.F., & Heimburge, J.A. (2007). *How to reach and teach all children through balanced literacy: User-friendly strategies, tools, activities, and ready-to-use materials. Grades 3–8.* **San Francisco: Jossey-Bass.**

This book offers a wide variety of engaging tools, tips, and strategies that are readily usable for the practicing teacher. Using a metaphor of literacy as an umbrella, the components of literacy instruction (reading, writing, speaking, and listening) are presented as inextricably connected. The book is broken down into 14 chapters, guiding the literacy practitioner through a veritable maze and serving as a how-to guide to taking a balanced literacy approach in the elementary and middle school classroom. Sprinkled throughout are ready-to-use reproducible student handouts, representing the authors' approach to strategic literacy instruction.

Start-to-Finish Publishing: Increase Reading Skills and Content Mastery

website: www.donjohnston.com/products/start_to_finish/index.html?gclid=CKGJktWk1pMCFQptswodakRqiQ

The universally designed Start-to-Finish Publishing series provides age-appropriate narrative and informational texts that are written at two readability levels and delivered in three media formats. Start-to-Finish Library offers a wide selection of engaging narrative chapter books for adolescent readers in the intermediate, middle, and high school grades who are not proficiently reading at grade level, and Start-to-Finish Core Content offers engaging, standards-based informational texts that prompt students to question, make meaning, and summarize as they read to learn in content area classes and intervention programs.

StoryPlace Pre-School Library

website: www.storyplace.org/preschool/other.asp

StoryPlace is an interactive digital library for younger and older children alike and features stories with various themes, such as animals, bath time, music, shapes, and trains. The website also includes online, take-home, and parent activities as well as suggested readings.

Teacher QuickSource

website: www.teacherquicksource.com

Preschool Activity QuickSource, a section of Teacher QuickSource by Excelligence Learning Corporation, is a comprehensive resource tailored to meet educators' specific needs and the needs of the children in their care. Early childhood teachers can find step-by-step activities, materials lists, and outcomes that correlate to NAEYC standards for Literacy in this site.

XYZ Is for Other

The final section of My ABCs includes several useful tools for planning and instruction (e.g., a guided participation framework), a reproducible weekly planner, and key sources of vocabulary words for teaching in the preschool years. These various items offer ideas and guidance in important areas of the preschool program.

Conversation Stretchers

Add Details

Teacher: What would you do if you found a dinosaur cave?

Child: I would leave it alone.

Teacher: Why would you leave it alone?

Child: 'Cause I don't want to bring it home.

Teacher: No?

Child: They would have to make a big door.

Teacher: A *gigantic* door.

Child: And a bigger house.

Explain Terms

Child: It was hot in here and that made all the water vaporate and that vaporation makes flowers droop.

Teacher: Yes, water evaporates from the soil when it's hot, and then the plan doesn't have enough. It wilts or droops.

Share Experiences

Teacher: So you went to the aquarium. When I went I was fascinated by the beautiful colors of the different small fishes.

Child: I saw a porpoise and the lady said they are NOT fish. They don't even have scales! Not everything that swims in the ocean is a fish, you know.

Wonder Aloud

Child: And I saw a ladybug beetle in my grandma's garden. She put ladybugs in her garden to eat aphids…yucky juice-suckers.

Teacher: I wonder if aphids are beetles? They weren't mentioned in the
beetle book we read. We should look that up.

Evaluation Checklist for Books, Toys, Websites, and Software

Books

Is the book age appropriate?

____ The children can relate the story to their lives and past experiences.

____ The children can identify with characters.

____ There is directly quoted conversation.

____ The children will benefit from the attitudes and models in the story.

Does the book teach early literacy?

____ The book can be used to expand knowledge.

____ There is new related vocabulary.

____ The book increases or broadens understanding.

____ The book is clearly written with a vocabulary and sequence that the children can understand.

____ Repetitions of words, actions, rhymes, or story parts are used.

____ The story structure is evident with a beginning, middle, and end.

____ The story includes humorous events and silly names.

What are some key criteria in choosing books?

____ The text is not too long to sit through.

____ There are not too many words to read.

____ There are enough colorful or action-packed pictures or illustrations to hold the children's attention.

____ The children can participate in the story by speaking or making actions.

____ The story is not too complex, symbolic, or confusing for the children.

Toys

Is the toy age appropriate?

____ The toy is the correct age level for the children.

____ Special instructions are not necessary to play with the toy.

____ Children cannot harm themselves unintentionally with the toy.

Does the toy teach early literacy?

___ The toy can be used in relation to storytelling.

___ The toy provides opportunities to expand vocabulary.

___ The toy has writing on it that correlates with actions being done.

___ There are opportunities for children to practice new vocabulary using the toy.

___ The toy increases or broadens understanding.

What are some key criteria in choosing toys?

___ The children are interested in the toy.

___ The toy is reusable.

___ The toy can be integrated into current or future lessons.

___ The toy is durable.

___ There are materials included with the toy for parents/teacher to use with the toy.

Websites and Software

Is the website or software age appropriate?

___ The children can understand the directions to use the website or software.

___ The instructions are easy to follow or relay to the children.

___ The website or software provides separate instructions for the parent or teacher.

Does the website or software teach early literacy?

___ The website or software can be used by the parent or teacher in a special way.

___ The website or software offers new vocabulary.

___ The website or software increases or broadens understanding.

___ The website or software is written clearly with a vocabulary and sequence that children can understand.

___ There are repetitions of words, actions, or rhymes.

___ The website or software has humorous parts and silly names.

What are some key criteria in choosing a proper website or software?

___ The parent or teacher enjoys using the website or software.

___ There are no confusing parts that the teacher or parent does not understand.

___ The children are able to follow the instructions with a parent or teacher present.

___ The website or software is challenging and provides opportunities for increasing skills.

Guided Participation Framework

Step One: Get Ready

___ Have materials out.

___ Sit near the children.

___ Get their attention.

___ Name what you will do.

___ Ask them to join in.

Step Two: Build Meaning

___ Help children join in.

___ Show them how.

___ Ask them to check their thinking.

___ Talk about what you are doing.

___ Help them succeed.

Step Three: Make Connections

___ Help children think about the activity.

___ Help them remember past experiences like it.

___ Ask them to predict what they will do.

___ Help them anticipate actions.

___ Encourage their ideas.

Step Four: Have Fun

___ Smile at the children.

___ Respond to their words and actions.

___ Show you care.

___ Laugh with them.

___ Enjoy the time spent.

Weekly Planner

Unit: _____

Last Theme: _____

Current Theme/Topic: _____

Next Theme: _____

Objectives:	Daily Schedule				
	Time	Activity	Grouping		
			Whole	Small Group	Center
		Getting Ready:			
		Circle I:			
		Shared Book Reading:			
		Day 1:			
		Day 2:			
		Days 3–5:			
		Center/Activity Time:			
Assessment(s):		Read-Alouds:			
Content Standards in This Theme:		Dramatic Play:			
		Writing:			
		Books:			
		Blocks:			
Home–School:		Discovery:			
		Art:			
		Circle II:			

Story Drama

Originally the technique of story drama was developed to prepare children for reading a story. But it can be adapted as a drama retell after a story is read. Basic procedures for each situation are provided here.

Before or After Reading a Story

- Tell the children the name of the story and discuss what it might be about OR after reading the story, discuss the main ideas.
- Select a number of key actions in the story (e.g., walking down a path). Read the section and have the children practice the movement.
- Establish the setting of the story by designating parts of the classroom as locations in the story.
- Divide the class into groups that represent characters in the story.
- Tell or read the story. Have each group "act out" its "character" part as the story is read. Direct children to locations as needed.

Source. Charters, J., & Gately, A. (1986). *Drama anytime.* Maryborough Vic, Australia: Primary English Teaching Association.

Vocabulary Sources

Biemiller, A. (2006). Vocabulary development and instruction: A prerequisite for school learning. In D.K. Dickinson & S.B. Neuman (Eds.), *Handbook of early literacy research* (Vol. 2, pp. 41–51). New York: Guilford.

Biemiller discusses vocabulary development and implications for academic success, including the relationship between early vocabulary and later literacy, the size and sequence of children's developing vocabulary, influence on vocabulary acquisition, and some mechanisms for word meaning acquisition. He also discusses what can be done to build vocabulary in schools and childcare programs, including reported effects of current schooling on vocabulary development, effects of teaching vocabulary to preschool or primary-grade children, a possible explanation of word meaning acquisition in context-based instruction, a basis for selecting words for instruction, a recent study of word instruction in classrooms, and practical implications for classroom programs.

Dale, E., & Chall, J. (1948). A formula for predicting readability.
Educational Research Bulletin, 27, 11–20, 37–54.

The new Dale–Chall readability formula calculates the U.S. grade level of a text sample based on sentence length and the number of unfamiliar words used in the sample. Unfamiliar words are ones that do not appear on a specially designed list of common words that are familiar to more than 80% of fourth-grade students. The original familiar word list included only 763 words; however, Professors Chall and Dale extended this list to 3,000 for the revised version of this formula in 1995. Because this formula is based on the usage of familiar words (rather than syllable or letter counts), it is often regarded as a more accurate test for younger readers.

Dolch, E.W. (1948). *Problems in reading.* Champaign, IL: The Garrard Press.

Based on an Interview Vocabulary study conducted by Dolch (1948), a topical analysis of words known in meaning to beginning first graders was made. Topics were derived from the Dale–Chall list and organized into topical groups considered relevant to child life (e.g., the body). Each topic contains subtopics that further define it as a category of meaning. The Child's Person, for example, includes the subtopics of body, senses, body actions, and clothes. Using the topical analysis, Dolch identified the *First Thousand Words for Children's Reading.* The 1,000-word collection provides a research-based vocabulary collection for early instruction.

REFERENCES

Adams, M.J. (1990). *Beginning to read: Thinking and learning about print*. Urbana: University of Illinois.

Adams, M.J., Foorman, B.R., Lundberg, I., & Beeler, T. (1998). *Phonemic awareness in young children: A classroom curriculum*. Baltimore: Paul H. Brookes.

Assel, M.A., Landry, S.H., Swank, P.R., & Gunnewig, S. (2007). An evaluation of curriculum, setting, and mentoring on the performance of children enrolled in pre-kindergarten. *Reading and Writing: An Interdisciplinary Journal, 20*(5), 463–494. doi:10.1007/s11145-006-9039-5

Beck, I.L., McKeown, M.G., & Kucan, L. (2002). *Bringing words to life: Robust vocabulary instruction*. New York: Guilford.

Biemiller, A. (2006). Vocabulary development and instruction: A prerequisite for school learning. In D.K. Dickinson & S.B. Neuman (Eds.), *Handbook of early literacy research* (Vol. 2, pp. 41–51). New York: Guilford.

Biemiller, A., & Slonim, N. (2001). Estimating root word vocabulary growth in normative and advantaged populations: Evidence for a common sequence of vocabulary acquisition. *Journal of Education & Psychology, 93*(3), 498–520. doi:10.1037/0022-0663.93.3.498

Blair, C. (2002). School readiness: Integrating cognition and emotion in a neurobiological conceptualization of children's functioning at school entry. *American Psychologist, 57*(2), 111–127. doi:10.1037/0003-066X.57.2.111

Bloom, P. (2000). *How children learn the meaning of words*. Cambridge, MA: MIT Press.

Bloom, P. (2002). Mindreading, communication, and the learning of the names for things. *Mind & Language, 17*(1&2), 37–54. doi:10.1111/1468-0017.00188

Bodrova, E., & Leong, D.J. (2007). *Tools of the mind: The Vygotskian approach to early childhood education*. Upper Saddle River, NJ: Pearson.

Bodrova, E., Leong, D.J., & Shore, R. (2004, March). Child outcome standards in pre-K programs: What are standards? What is needed to make them work? *Preschool Policy Matters*. Retrieved October 21, 2008, from nieer.org/resources/policybriefs/5.pdf

Bowman, B.T., Donovan, S., & Burns, M.S. (2001). *Eager to learn: Educating our preschoolers*. Washington, DC: National Academy Press.

Breneman, L.N., & Breneman, B. (1983). *Once upon a time: A storytelling handbook*. Chicago: Nelson-Hall.

Bruner, J.S. (1983). *Child's talk: Learning to use language*. New York: Norton.

Burgess, S.R. (2006). The development of phonological sensitivity. In D.K. Dickinson & S.B. Neuman (Eds.), *Handbook of early literacy research* (Vol. 2, pp. 90–100). New York: Guilford.

Bus, A.G., & Both-de Vries, A.C. (2008, March). *Name writing as a catalyst for phonemic awareness.* Paper presented by the American Educational Research Association, New York, NY.

California Department of Education. (2007). *Preschool English learners: Principles and practices to promote language, literacy, and learning.* Sacramento: Author.

Chall, J.S. (1983). *Stages of reading development.* New York: McGraw-Hill.

Chall, J.S. (1996). *Stages of reading development* (2nd ed.). Fort Worth, TX: Harcourt College.

Charters, J., & Gately, A. (1986). *Drama anytime.* Portsmouth, NH: Heinemann Educational Books.

Christie, J.F., & Roskos, K. (2006). Standards, science, and the role of play in early literacy education. In D.G. Singer, R.M. Golinkoff, & K. Hirsh-Pasek (Eds.), *Play=learning: How play motivates and enhances children's cognitive and social-emotional growth* (pp. 57–73). Oxford, UK: Oxford University Press.

Diamond, A., Barnett, W.S., Thomas, J., & Munro, S. (2007). Preschool program improves cognitive control. *Science, 318*(5855), 1387–1388. doi:10.1126/science.1151148

Dickinson, D.K., McCabe, A., & Sprague, K. (2003). Teacher rating of oral language and literacy (TROLL): Individualizing early literacy instruction with a standards-based rating tool. *The Reading Teacher, 56*(6), 554–564.

Dickinson, D.K., & Neuman, S.B. (Eds.). (2006). *Handbook of early literacy research* (Vol. 2). New York: Guilford.

Dickinson, D.K., & Tabors, P.O. (2001). *Beginning literacy with language: Young children learning at home and school.* Baltimore: Paul H. Brookes.

Edwards, C.P., Gandini, L., & Forman G.E. (Eds.). (1998). *The hundred languages of children: The Reggio Emilia approach—Advanced reflections* (2nd ed.). Greenwich, CT: Ablex.

Ehri, L.C., & Roberts, T. (2006). The roots of learning to read and write: Acquisition of letters and phonemic awareness. In D.K. Dickinson & S.B. Neuman (Eds.), *Handbook of early literacy research* (Vol. 2, pp. 113–131). New York: Guilford.

Ergul, C., Burstein, K., Bryan, T., & Christie, J. (2007, April). *Addressing the early literacy development of young ELL in a scientifically-based preschool program.* Paper presented at American Educational Research Association, Chicago, IL.

Goswami, U. (2001). Early phonological development and the acquisition of literacy. In S.B. Neuman & D.K. Dickinson (Eds.), *Handbook of early literacy research* (pp. 111–125). New York: Guilford.

Halliday, M.A.K. (1977). *Learning how to mean: Explorations in the development of language.* New York: Elsevier.

Hart, B., & Risley, T. (2003). The early catastrophe: The 30 million word gap. *American Educator, 27*(1), 4–9.

Hawley, W., & Valli, L. (1999). The essentials of effective professional development: A new consensus. In L. Darling-Hammond & G. Sykes (Eds.), *Teaching as the learning profession: Handbook of policy and practice* (pp. 127–150). San Francisco: Jossey-Bass.

Hirsch, E.D., Jr. (2003). Reading comprehension requires knowledge—of words and the world. *American Educator, 27*(1), 10–29.

Holdaway, D. (1979). *The foundations of literacy.* Portsmouth, NH: Heinemann.

Johnson, J.E., Christie, J.F., & Wardle, F. (2005). *Play, development, and early education.* Boston: Allyn & Bacon.

Kaderavek, J., & Justice, L.M. (2002). Shared storybook reading as an intervention context: Practices and potential pitfalls. *American Journal of Speech-Language Pathology, 11*(4), 395–406.

Mardell, B. (1999). *From basketball to the Beatles: In search of compelling early childhood curriculum.* Portsmouth, NH: Heinemann.

McGee, L.M., & Richgels, D.J. (2003). *Designing early literacy programs: Strategies for at-risk preschool and kindergarten children.* New York: Guilford.

Morris, D. (1992). *Case studies in teaching beginning readers: The Howard Street tutoring manual.* Boone, NC: Fieldstream Publications.

Neuman, S.B., & Roskos, K.A. (1989). Preschoolers' conceptions of literacy as reflected in their spontaneous play. In S. McCormick, J. Zutell, P. Scharer, & P.R. Okeefe (Eds.), *Cognitive and social perspective for literacy research and instruction* (38th yearbook of the National Reading Conference, pp. 87–94). Chicago: National Reading Conference.

Neuman, S.B., & Roskos, K.A. (1993). Access to print for children of poverty: Differential effects of adult mediation and literacy-enriched play settings on environmental and functional print tasks. *American Educational Research Journal, 30*(1), 95–122.

Neuman, S.B., & Roskos, K.A. (2007). *Nurturing knowledge: Building a foundation for school success by linking early literacy to math, science, art and social studies.* New York: Scholastic.

New Standards Speaking and Listening Committee. (2001). *Speaking and listening for preschool through third grade.* Washington, DC: National Center on Education and the Economy and the University of Pittsburgh.

Newmann, F.M. (Ed.). (1998). *Authentic achievement: Restructuring schools for intellectual quality.* San Francisco: Jossey-Bass.

Robbins, C., & Ehri, L.C. (1994). Reading storybooks to kindergartners helps them learn new vocabulary words. *Journal of Educational Psychology, 86*(1), 54–64. doi:10.1037/0022-0663.86.1.54

Roskos, K.A. (2008, May). *Efficacy of a vocabulary instruction protocol in preschool programs.* Paper presented at the International Reading Conference, Atlanta, GA.

Roskos, K.A., & Christie, J.F. (2007). *Play and literacy in early childhood: Research from multiple perspectives* (2nd ed.). Mahwah, NJ: Erlbaum.

Saville-Troike, M. (1987). Bilingual discourse: The negotiation of meaning without a common code. *Linguistics, 25,* 81–106.

Scarborough, H.S. (2001). Connecting early language and literacy to later reading (dis)abilities: Evidence, theory, and practice. In S.B. Neuman & D.K. Dickinson (Eds.), *Handbook of early literacy research* (pp. 97–110). New York: Guilford.

Sénéchal, M. (1997). The differential effect of storybook reading on preschoolers' acquisition of expressive and receptive vocabulary. *Journal of Child Language, 24*(1), 123–138. doi:10.1017/S0305000996003005

Sénéchal, M., & Cornell, E.H. (1993). Vocabulary acquisition through shared reading experiences. *Reading Research Quarterly, 28*(4), 360–376. doi:10.2307/747933

Singer, D.G., & Singer, J.L. (1990). *The house of make-believe: Children's play and developing imagination.* Cambridge, MA: Harvard University Press.

Smith, P.K. (2007). Pretend play and children's cognitive and literacy development: Sources of evidence and some lessons from the past. In K.A. Roskos & J.F. Christie (Eds.), *Play and literacy in early childhood: Research from multiple perspectives* (pp. 3–20). Mahwah, NJ: Erlbaum.

Snow, C.E., Burns, M.S., & Griffin P. (Eds.). (1998). *Preventing reading difficulties in young children.* Washington, DC: National Academy Press.

Soderman, A.K., Gregory, K.M., & O'Neill, L.T. (1999). *Scaffolding emergent literacy: A child-centered approach for preschool through grade 5.* Columbus, OH: Merrill.

Stahl, S.A. (2003). How words are learned incrementally over multiple exposures. *American Educator, 27*(1), 18–19, 44.

Stanovich, K.E. (2000). *Progress in understanding reading: Scientific foundations and new frontiers.* New York: Guilford.

Tabors, P.O. (2008). *One child, two languages: A guide for early childhood educators of children learning English as a second language* (2nd ed.). Baltimore: Paul H. Brookes.

Tough, J. (1981). *A place for talk: The role of talk in the education of the children with moderate learning difficulties.* London: Ward Lock Educational.

U.S. Department of Health and Human Services. (2003). *The Head Start path to positive child outcomes* [The Head Start Child Outcomes Framework]. Retrieved May 18, 2004, from www.hsnrc.org/CDI/outcontent.cfm

Vukelich, C., Christie, J.F., & Enz, B. (2002). *Helping young children learn language and literacy.* Boston: Allyn & Bacon.

Vygotsky, L.S. (1962). *Thought and language* (E. Hanfmann & G. Vokar, Trans.). Cambridge, MA: MIT Press. (Original work published 1934)

Wagner, R.K., & Torgeson, J.K. (1987). The nature of phonological processing and its causal role in the acquisition of reading skills. *Psychological Bulletin, 101*(2), 192–212. doi:10.1037/0033-2909.101.2.192

Wells, G. (1986). *The meaning makers: Children learning language and using language to learn.* Portsmouth, NH: Heinemann.

Wolf, M. (1991). Naming speed and reading: The contribution of the cognitive neurosciences. *Reading Research Quarterly, 26*(2), 123–141. doi:10.2307/747978

Wong Fillmore, L. (1979). Individual differences in second language acquisition. In C.J. Fillmore, D. Kempler, & W. Wang (Eds.), *Individual differences in language ability and language behavior* (pp. 203–228). New York: Academic.

Wood, D.J., McMahon, L., & Cranstoun, Y. (1980). *Working with under fives.* London: Grant McIntyre.

CHILDREN'S LITERATURE CITED

Arnosky, J. (2001). *Raccoon on his own*. New York: Puffin.

Gibbons, G. (1996). *Cats*. New York: Scholastic.

Goldin, A.R. (1965). *Ducks don't get wet*. Toronto: Fitzhenry & Whiteside Limited.

Henkes, K. (1996). *Lilly's purple plastic purse*. New York: Greenwillow.

Lee, D. (2002). *Sylvia's garage*. Bothell, WA: Wright Group.

Martin, B. (1996). *Brown bear, brown bear, what do you see?* New York: Henry Holt.

Ottolenghi, C. (2001). *The little red hen*. San Francisco: Brighter Child.

Perkins, A. (1968). *The ear book*. New York: Random House.

Resnick, J.P. (1996). *Spiders*. Chicago: Kidsbooks.

Rey, H.A. (1941). *Curious George*. Boston: Houghton Mifflin.

Willems, M. (2004). *Knuffle Bunny: A cautionary tale*. New York: Hyperion.

Wood, A. (1984). *The napping house*. San Diego, CA: Harcourt.

INDEX

Note: Page numbers followed by *f* and *t* indicate figures and tables, respectively.

C

W